The authors are sisters who have studied the medical and legal issues surrounding end-of-life policy since it first began to surface at conferences and in academic journals in the 1980s. DR. JEANNE FITZPATRICK has practiced emergency medicine in small cities and rural areas around the country for over twenty-five years. She currently lives outside of Salem, Oregon, and works in the Emergency Department at Santiam Memorial Hospital in Stayton, Oregon. EILEEN M. FITZPATRICK, a graduate of Harvard Law School, practiced corporate law in Boston prior to moving to rural New England to pursue a career in writing. She lives in Dana Point, California, where she is active in local politics.

"A thoughtful and heartfelt book that exposes an alarming truth about end-of-life care in America, one that every physician who has cared for the dying knows: Even when patients do everything 'right' to assure that these intensely personal preferences are honored, there's still much that can go wrong. Intent on preventing such injustices, the authors have articulated a pragmatic step-by-step approach you can use to make sure this doesn't happen to you. I'll be sharing this book with many patients."

—Mark Lachs, MD, MPH, Professor of Medicine, Weill Medical College of Cornell University

Lovingly and gratefully dedicated to
Craig Wesley Fitzpatrick and Lois Fitzpatrick Briley

Contents

WHO CAN USE THE COMPASSION PROTOCOL   45

CHAPTER THREE

THE COMPETENT ELDERLY   47

CHAPTER FOUR

THE TERMINALLY ILL   65

CHAPTER FIVE

ALZHEIMER'S DEMENTIA AND THE COMPASSION PROTOCOL   85

HOW THE COMPASSION PROTOCOL WORKS   103

CHAPTER SIX

STEP ONE: KNOW YOUR OPTIONS   107

Foreword

Consider for a moment how unusual in many ways are the questions raised in *A Better Way of Dying*.

Go back just forty years ago, and there were no Living Wills, no health care powers of attorney, no 911 to call, no diagnosis of persistent vegetative state/permanent unconsciousness, no state laws defining "death," nothing called a DNR order. (In 1966, the National Academy of Sciences first recommended that doctors begin learning a new technique called CPR. The very idea of any need to pair the words "do not" with "resuscitate" was decades away.) Back then the issues addressed by this book did not yet exist. Seriously ill patients took all the treatment the doctor had to offer, and either got better or died. No questions about the appropriateness of treatment were needed or asked. All treatment available was given and accepted gladly.

The rapid advance of medical technology has changed that dynamic forever. That change, on balance, is of course for the good. Americans are not only living longer, but we are also thriving as we age. And with that thriving has come a new set of circumstances at the end of our lives. Dying happens differently today than it did forty years ago. The idea of letting nature take its course has fallen by the wayside from both the medical and technological perspectives. Most deaths now happen in institutions, and most are the result of a decision—antibiotics refused, respirators turned off, feeding tubes clamped. And while the technology that keeps us alive grows ever more complex, the questions about when it is appropriate to use that technology are in many ways basic, fundamental human questions that all of us will benefit from discussing: What is the purpose of medicine? When do we use it? And when should we stop?

Interestingly, though perhaps not surprisingly, much of the societal discussion about how we navigate decisions at the end of life has played out through our legal system. I have been involved in that discussion since the spring of 1987, when I became the lawyer for Nancy Cruzan and her family. Nancy's tragic case ultimately ended up in the U.S. Supreme Court, where in 1990 the Court established the right of Americans to make decisions about our own medical care, including whether we have the right to refuse treatment—what some call our "right to die."

The law, however, is not the best venue to develop good decision making in medicine, since it typically scrambles to keep pace with science and technology. That truism certainly applies at the end of life. Legislators in Missouri who passed our first Living Will law in 1985 believed they were "solving" cases like Nancy Cruzan's. So did federal lawmakers who passed the Patient Self-Determination Act in 1990. Various efforts in other states—health care powers of attorney, out-of-hospital DNR rules, decision-hierarchy laws—have all been aimed at such "solving." There is no question that these laws give us tools, structure, rights, and guidance. But none of them can really resolve the hard, multifaceted questions we face at the end of life. The law is black and white, and those questions exist deep in the gray zones of society, where answers are seldom simple.

Yet answers to the questions do exist. This suggestion may sound way too simplistic, but after spending years working on end-of-life issues, I'm convinced that our society will find the answers if we simply do a better job of talking with one another. Medical studies support this admittedly basic proposition. They show that patients who talk with their families and doctors end up with fewer unwanted ER and ICU visits in their final months of life. These patients often choose home care and hospice instead. They and their families routinely report higher satisfaction with the less technological path. And, perhaps surprising to many, various studies suggest that patients live about as long whether they choose the high-technological path of the hospital, home care, hospice, or other paths of less technological care.

In short, talking about our dying improves how we die.

Which brings me to *A Better Way of Dying*. In this book Dr. Jeanne Fitzpatrick and attorney Eileen Fitzpatrick develop a thorough and interesting new approach to facilitating that societal discussion. Using compelling stories of patients taken from Dr. Fitzpatrick's practice of many years, they provide a detailed road map for talking about end-of-life care—one that includes Alzheimer's disease, nursing homes, feeding tubes, and many of the hard questions that modern medical technology is bringing to our society.

Do your loved ones a favor. Read *A Better Way of Dying*. Talk about the stories you encounter in the book. Expand the discussion about what you've learned beyond your loved ones—to your doctor and minister and to others in your social circle who will care about how medical decisions might be made for you if accident or illness leaves you unable to speak on your own behalf. Write down who it is that you want to speak for you should this happen, and then arm that person to act as your advocate—for less treatment, more treatment, or different treatment.

What is the purpose of medicine? When do we use it? And when should we stop? Sharing your own answers to these questions is a gift to those you love. The stories in this book will help you give that gift. So, let's talk.

William Colby
Senior Fellow, Law and Patient Rights
Center for Practical Bioethics
www.PracticalBioethics.org
March 25, 2009

Prologue

ATTORNEY EILEEN FITZPATRICK

My sister, Dr. Jeanne Fitzpatrick, has a remarkable story to tell. She has worked as an emergency room physician in small, mostly rural towns in Alaska, Washington, Oregon, Hawaii, and New Mexico.

Unlike ER doctors on television, she rarely deals with multiple gunshot wounds or catastrophic freeway pileups. Instead, as many as a third of her patients are from local nursing homes—the infirm elderly, the demented, and the terminally ill.

Jeanne sees many patients who have exhausted their enjoyment of life and want to die and who have even signed legal papers to that effect, but who are kept alive in a lingering state of suffering despite their clearly expressed wishes.

When I raise the subject of our book with people, I invariably hear a story of an unpleasant or drawn-out death in the family. One person's great aunt was force-fed when she broke her hip at the age of eighty-seven, decided it was time to go, and stopped eating. Another had a grandmother whose nursing home refused to disconnect her respirator, though she was brain-dead, until the Medicaid payments ran out.

Everyone, it seems, has a story that reinforces our observation: Death in the modern world is often an unnecessarily prolonged and painful event accompanied by medical technology that separates a dying person from the community in which he or she lives. While most of us clearly state that we would prefer to die at home in our own beds, 80 percent of us die in hospitals or nursing homes.

As an attorney, I have noted how often nursing homes and other caregivers ignore patients' legal directives and needlessly prolong suffering at the end of life. Our book takes an open, honest look at this problem and offers a simple-to-follow five-step Compassion Protocol that people can follow in making the decision to cease medical intervention and allow a natural death to occur.

The Compassion Protocol does not rely solely on legal forms to get results. Of course, Advance Directive forms are necessary, but legal forms are dry, static things that cannot hope to define the parameters of an event as individual and dynamic as death. Rather, our solution is communication-based and offers a series of integrative steps that anyone can follow for approaching life's final event.

Death, this one certainty of life, inevitable and unavoidable, should not be hidden in the closet of social unmentionables. Many of us are dealing with our parents' end-of-life issues: debility, dementia, nursing homes—the slow decline into dependence.

The current social and medical response to these issues often produces protracted pain and suffering. My sister and I know we can do better, and we invite you to join us in restoring natural death to its rightful place among treatment options at the end of life.

DR. JEANNE FITZPATRICK

This book is the distillation of five years of reflection and a lifetime of experience and insight. During that time I have talked to many people—patients, other health care workers, family, friends—about the subject of death. When I say my lawyer-sister and I are writing a book about dying, most look away and change the subject. But when I continue and tell them we are writing about how to avoid a long, slow decline in a nursing home, their attitudes change quickly. Often, the response is "Send me a copy!"

More and more people are realizing that they would prefer death over clinging to a life of pain, debility, and dependence. Of course, there are those who believe every available medical intervention must be used to extend life as long as possible. We say, more power to you—but this book is for the rest of us.

For those people more interested in quality of life than quantity, we offer a straightforward plan for achieving a natural death when you are ready. Our Compassion Protocol offers five simple steps which ensure that when you are at the end of your life, you can choose to be allowed a "natural death."

What do we mean by a natural death? If you rule out homicide and suicide, all other deaths are from natural causes. But some deaths are more natural than others. From antibiotics to the latest gene therapies, advances in medicine have both increased our life span and brought relief from common ailments. Modern medicine can keep us alive a really long time, which is a good thing—except when it isn't.

In this book we use *natural death* to refer to dying from an illness or infection that a patient chooses not to have treated because that patient felt it was time to die.

Sound radical? It may, but the idea has some precedent in other areas of medicine. Natural childbirth was a radical change from maximum to minimum medical intervention in the processes of birth. As a result of the "natural childbirth" movement, childbirth as a life event was rethought and literally reconstructed so as to minimize stress on the infant, mother, and father.

Our country has been on the verge of a "natural death" movement since the late 1970s. Some progress has been made with advances such as the growth of hospice care and the advent of Do Not Resuscitate (DNR) orders. But all too often people still do not get the timely natural death they would prefer, as the stories in this book illustrate and statistical evidence supports.

My sister and I wrote this book to bridge the gap between the way most of us would prefer to experience the end of life and the way modern medicine treats the dying. Our Compassion Protocol offers a concrete way to say, "Enough. Let me die," when you are ready to let natural death occur.

In the first few chapters I relate how a number of my patients educated me about death and dying. Included are stories of deaths I have observed as well as stories of some patients who had clearly expressed a desire to die, by means of a DNR order or other document, but were not allowed to do so.

These experiences convinced me that natural death must be reintroduced as an option for the end of life. It is my hope that the stories also honor the patients who were my teachers.

DEATH AND DYING
IN AMERICA

SECTION ONE

DEATH AND DYING
IN AMERICA

CHAPTER ONE

The Need for Change: The Cautionary Tale of Phyllis Shattuck

Nestled in the heart of rural Pennsylvania is a renowned regional teaching hospital with a prominent postgraduate training program in medical specialties. Here Dr. Fitzpatrick was in her tenth month of residency on an internal medicine rotation—by far the hardest rotation of a difficult year. The death of Phyllis Shattuck would fill these six weeks with memorable lessons that have followed Dr. Fitzpatrick throughout her life.

DR. FITZPATRICK TELLS PHYLLIS SHATTUCK'S STORY

I met Phyllis Shattuck at 2:30 in the morning in the Emergency Room. So far during my residency, sleep was like strawberry shortcake: something rarely encountered but still a distinct and longed-for experience. Residents served twenty-four-hour shifts every third day, catching naps when the work was slow. Exhaustion was a routine and expected part of the first year of residency, and I had been on duty, and mostly awake, every third night for much of the year.

I had just fallen asleep after a busy night when the phone rang to summon me back to the ER. The nurse told me an ambulance was on its way in with a patient described as "a fifty-seven-year-old woman with end-stage lung cancer, in respiratory distress." As I rushed down the two flights of stairs from the on-call sleeping cubicle to the ER, my brain struggled to remember the basics of treatment for acute respiratory distress. Would I be intubating* this person?

I Meet the Players in This Drama

When I first saw Phyllis, she was sitting forward on the bed—a thin, frail woman fighting for breath. I recognized her "three-point stance"; the weight of her chest supported by her straight arms so all of her chest muscles could work at breathing. Her nose tipped toward the ceiling in the "sniffing" posture, straightening her airway to provide the least resistance to incoming air. Her eyes reflected her exhaustion. In her world all that mattered was breathing.

Beside her stood Robert, her husband of thirty-five years. He was an immovable rock, holding his hat in his right hand, his left hand resting lightly on Phyllis's shoulder. He said, "We were here two weeks ago. They sent us home and said there's nothing else they can do for her. But she couldn't breathe at home. I couldn't see her suffer so. She shouldn't have to be so miserable, just wanting to breathe."

I would get to know Robert well in the next six weeks, well

---

*   Many of the medical terms used in this book are defined in the glossary.

enough to know that this was a lengthy statement for him. He had been studying how to tell the doctor why he and Phyllis were here, and this was the most detailed summary of the situation he could muster.

I took Phyllis's pulse and noted her labored breathing, her color, and the sunken, absent look to her eyes. I knew she was at the end of an illness that was going to kill her—and soon, from the look of things.

EASY TO SAY, IMPOSSIBLE TO DO

Phyllis struggled to focus, getting out two or three words on each breath: "I wanted to die at home. Please just let me die. It's my time, and I'm ready. I'm just so tired of it all." She closed her eyes then and laid her head back on the gurney to rest. This bed, like most in the ER, had no pillow.

She was getting high-flow oxygen from a mask over her nose and mouth, giving her 10 liters of oxygen per minute. I asked Robert if she had oxygen at home.

"No. She's doing much better just from having that on. She couldn't talk at home and kept getting confused and slipping away. It seems like the oxygen helps a lot."

Phyllis's eyes were closed now, and she had slipped into unconsciousness. Having end-stage lung cancer meant she had benefited as much as she would from treatment, whether surgery, chemotherapy, or radiation. There was no hope that she would return to a long and productive life. Her cancer would kill her.

More immediately, high-flow oxygen could kill her if she had underlying lung disease. Most people breathe not because they need oxygen but because they need to exhale carbon dioxide. This need to get rid of carbon dioxide is called our hypercarbic drive, the brain's stimulus to breathe triggered by a buildup of carbon dioxide. It is a much stronger drive than hypoxia, or low oxygen in the blood, which stimulates breathing when the oxygen content in the body gets too low.

Chronic lungers—those with bad emphysema, asthma, or chronic bronchitis—retain carbon dioxide and turn off their hypercarbic drive. Hypoxia is their only stimulus to breathe and especially to work hard at breathing. Phyllis's lung disease had destroyed her hypercarbic drive, and she came in gasping for breath because she couldn't get enough oxygen.

In short, Phyllis was having a potential exit event—that is, a naturally occurring illness that, left untreated, would probably cause death. With the high-flow oxygen we were giving her, Phyllis's breathing was slowing as her body filled with oxygen. Her hypoxic drive was temporarily satisfied even as her carbon dioxide was probably climbing. Giving Phyllis lots of oxygen would suppress her hypoxic drive to breathe, and her carbon dioxide, already at a chronically high level, would climb slowly but steadily until it reached a level that was toxic to her heart.

If nothing was done, Phyllis's heart would soon go into a dysrhythmia and eventually arrest. The only way to stop this process was to intubate her and put her on a ventilator.

Phyllis had just stated that she wanted to die with no intervention. It was my job in the next crucial twenty minutes to decide whether to start Phyllis on life support or grant her wish to die peacefully and comfortably. Or so I thought.

ENTER DR. "MY PATIENTS DON'T DIE" HASTINGS

At that point two nurses entered the room. One of them pushed Robert aside on her way to the head of the bed. "Mrs. Shattuck," she said from behind her patient, unaware that Phyllis had slipped into a coma, "we're going to put in an IV and draw a blood gas." The other nurse hovered at the side of the bed with a tray of blood tubes.

I spoke up. "Wait. I'm not sure that's what we want to do."

The nurse at the head of the bed stopped and looked at me. "Who are you?" she asked.

"I'm Dr. Fitzpatrick, the medicine service admitting doc. Mrs. Shattuck is my patient. I'm just evaluating her."

"No. She's Dr. Hastings's patient," the nurse said. "He knows she's here, and he called in some orders. He said she'll probably go on a ventilator, and anesthesia's on their way over, I just called them."

"Who's Dr. Hastings?" I asked.

Robert stepped forward now and said, "He's her doctor. When she went unconscious on me at home, I called him, and he told me to call the ambulance and bring her right in. So that's how we got here."

Ignoring Robert, the nurse answered, "He's her attending. He's already given a bunch of orders. Maybe you ought to talk to him." The nurse resumed her work, getting ready to start the IV. The lab tech was drawing blood.

I stood there, still holding Phyllis's hand, watching the door to a quagmire open in front of me. I felt I knew the right action, but I watched the moment slip away, feeling powerless to call it back.

FIRST, DO NO HARM

The room got more crowded as the respiratory therapist wheeled in the EKG machine. I stepped back as he bared Phyllis's chest and began hooking up electrodes. The X-ray technician had arrived with the portable X-ray machine and was waiting her turn. Phyllis remained asleep or in a coma through all this.

"Robert, could I talk to you outside? Robert?" I had to repeat his name a couple of times to get his attention, but he eventually headed out the door with me. From the doorway he looked back at Phyllis, now buried behind all the people.

I took his arm and led him to a quiet corner of the ER. It was 2 a.m., and there was little activity. Robert moved slowly, implacable, oblivious to his surroundings. He stared at the floor, and I said to his bowed head, "Your wife's not doing very well."

He turned his hat in his hands. "I know. She's dying. We've been getting ready for it. She's suffered a lot, and she's ready to go."

I felt like screaming, "But they're not going to let her die. They're in there doing things to her specifically to keep her from dying." I held my tongue and took a deep breath.

This was not the first time I had been caught in this dilemma. The hospital I was working at was a tertiary care facility, the referral hospital for all of central Pennsylvania. This meant it received patients whom no one else could cure. A high percentage of patients were at the end of their lives and came to this hospital looking for a miracle. Most of them didn't find one, and many of them left through the morgue. How much to do, how aggressively to treat, and when to pull the plug were decisions that I had been making all year.

Three months earlier, while on hematology rotation, I received a patient in the middle of the night. The patient had been diagnosed by her doctor two weeks earlier with an advanced stage of leukemia. She was sent to us because a very low platelet count had caused a massive bleed into her brain. She came with a CT brain scan showing that the bleed had filled half of her brain, which was swelling and pushing on the other half. She was deeply unresponsive with very poor vital signs and had no chance of recovery based on the brain damage already shown on the CT. In view of her very poor prognosis, I decided to keep her comfortable and do little to intervene. She died about four hours later, in a comfortable bed with her sister by her side. The attending doctor tried to have me terminated from the residency because the patient had no IV and wasn't transfused with platelets. He could not explain to me how either of those actions would have mattered to the patient or affected the outcome, but he was furious with me for not doing them.

Did Phyllis have any chance of finding a quiet and peaceful death in the hospital that night? That appeared to be her wish. Phyllis had already suffered a great deal, had no hope of anything but more suffering in the future, and had stated unequivocally that she just wanted merciful release.

A WISE MAN KNOWS HIS OWN EXIT EVENT

By this time in my residency I had watched other terminal patients reach the point where their suffering overwhelmed their will to live and they became ready to die. Many of them experienced a possible exit event during their hospital stay. I had seen many terminal patients coming into the hospital over and over again for treatment of illnesses that might have been exit events, and this was even after the patient was ready to die. They would stay for a week for curative treatment of their acute illness and then return to their life of suffering.

I had also taken care of those who were lost in a maze of dementia or brain damage from a stroke, long past the point of making their own decisions. These patients had also not been allowed to successfully utilize an exit event to end their suffering.

Even when we know the patient is at the end of life with an incurable illness and is in a miserable condition with no chance of improvement, modern medical protocol requires doctors to cure any other ailment that can be cured, keeping the patient alive as long as possible with no consideration for his or her quality of life.

Even most Advance Directives do not go so far as allowing doctors to withhold simple curative treatment of pneumonia or other infections in someone who is ready to die. Where the Advance Directive does allow a doctor to withhold antibiotics for pneumonia, it is interpreted that it applies only when the patient is in a coma. This practice has always seemed wrong to me because it totally discounts and disrespects the patient's (often explicitly stated) wishes. Phyllis was definitely experiencing an exit event with an opportunity for a quiet, peaceful death—and that opportunity was about to be denied.

Both Robert and Phyllis had told me unequivocally that Phyllis was ready to die. I decided to try to help Phyllis avoid intubation, a procedure I felt would only prolong her misery. I talked to Robert about it but hit a wall often encountered with families of the dying. Not having done the difficult mental and emotional work necessary to prepare for the inevitable end, Robert was unprepared to make the final choices his loved one had requested.

"Robert, has Phyllis ever been on a ventilator before, where the machine breathes for her?"

"Yes. The last three or four times she's been in the hospital she needed that. The last time, just last month, she was on it for two weeks. She was miserable. That's when they said they couldn't do anything else for her, and we knew she was going to die."

"They're planning to put her on the breathing machine again right now. If they don't, she'll die very soon—within a few hours. Do you think she wants to be on the breathing machine again?"

This was a decision Robert couldn't make. He was faced with the imminent death of his wife, and his mind was busy trying to imagine a life without her and thinking about the millions of ways in which life was about to change. He wasn't listening to me and was unable to make a difficult decision at this critical juncture.

SO MANY DOCTORS, SO LITTLE CARE

Although Phyllis's doctors had told her that death was imminent and unavoidable, they were still ordering life-prolonging medical care that could only extend her suffering. Like many of the terminal patients I had seen that year, Phyllis was betrayed by the medical system in the following ways:

- Phyllis's attending doctor did not provide Phyllis and Robert with a referral for end-of-life counseling.

- Phyllis and Robert were unaware of both the timetable for Phyllis's death and the various medical interventions possible to prolong her life.
- Phyllis was sent home to die without any concern for her comfort; she lacked simple oxygen and pain medication that would have allowed her to remain at home with her family.
- Phyllis and Robert were unaware that they could make decisions that might positively impact Phyllis's end-of-life experience.

At a loss and totally unprepared to make this decision, Robert said, "Dr. Hastings probably knows what's best for her." Phyllis's wishes were swept away by the routine response of the medical system: Prolong life at any cost.

SEEKING A REVERSIBLE COMPONENT

I stayed with Phyllis as much as I could that night. The anesthesiologist came, intubated her, and placed her on a ventilator. He put in an arterial line, a permanent tube in her wrist so they could check blood gases without having to poke a new hole in an artery every time. This meant her right arm was tied down so that she couldn't dislodge the arterial line. She was heavily sedated by the anesthesiologist, so she would just let the machine breathe for her and not fight against it.

She surfaced to consciousness once briefly during the night, about three hours after she was intubated. She couldn't communicate with the tube in her lungs, but the tears in her eyes spoke her feelings.

By the next afternoon, twelve hours after Phyllis's arrival, the ventilator had cleared her blood of the carbon dioxide and she was fully awake and alert. She was requiring high PEEP (positive end-expiratory pressure) and high oxygen settings on the ventilator just to maintain adequate blood gases.

The note from the anesthesiologist, who saw her about an hour before I did, read: "I anticipate extreme difficulty getting this patient off the ventilator." There was also a note from Dr. Hastings. He wrote, "Patient with end-stage lung cancer, near respiratory arrest, intubated to allow treatment of any reversible component. Expect poor outcome." A reversible component would be a treatable illness that could be fixed in order to keep Phyllis alive longer—some spasm in the bronchial muscles, a buildup of secretions, an infection—something that, when reversed, would make breathing easier for Phyllis. Dr. Hastings *might* have expected such a reversible component; I suspect he just found it easier to put Phyllis on a ventilator than to deal with her death.

AND DITCH THE CHALKBOARD

During the morning someone had gotten Phyllis a chalkboard and piece of chalk so she could communicate. She had it ready when I walked in and turned it around for me to read. "PLEASE LET ME DIE," it said in large letters. Phyllis watched with angry eyes while I read it.

I knew immediately how miserably I had failed to provide

this woman with the only thing she wanted from me. I sat next to Phyllis on the bed and took her hands. Phyllis's face crumpled, the anger replaced by incredible sadness, while her eyes filled with tears again.

I said, inadequately, "I'm so sorry, Phyllis. Dr. Hastings thought this was the best thing for you. I couldn't fight him; he's my boss."

Phyllis took her chalk, underlined the four words on the board, added two exclamation marks, and shoved the board at me. She pointed to my heart and poked my chest with her pointed finger. You, you, she was saying in the only way she could, please let me die.

THE LAST WORD

Phyllis stayed alive on the ventilator for six weeks. For her it was six weeks of misery. Each day her doctors tried to wean her off the ventilator, lowering the oxygen supplied by the machine until Phyllis's hypoxic drive kicked in. She would then pant and struggle for air, just as she had when she arrived in the ER, until she became too fatigued. When her carbon dioxide rose to a dangerous level, they would turn the ventilator back up again.

With her breathing controlled, her body suffered from the increasing effects of her metastatic cancer. She became weaker as her body wasted away. She received Total Parenteral Nutrition (TPN), an IV solution designed to support life in someone who can't eat. But this didn't stop her muscles from wasting as the cancer built up toxins in her body.

For six weeks she greeted me each day with the note written on her chalkboard, "PLEASE LET ME DIE."

I made a point of being there one day when Dr. Hastings made his rounds. When Phyllis showed him the blackboard with its very clear message, he said to her, "Now, Phyllis, you're not going to die. Don't be silly. We'll get your lungs opened up and get you off this machine and home."

When I tried to raise the subject of Phyllis's death with Dr. Hastings, he said to me, "My patients don't die."

For Phyllis's first two weeks Dr. Hastings continued to talk about "treating the reversible component" of her lung cancer, getting her off the machine, and sending her home. He said little about her in the two weeks after that. She had been there for four weeks, in the ICU, on the ventilator, before he first theorized about what organ might fail next to cause her death: her heart or maybe her kidneys.

Meanwhile, he checked tests daily to be sure some minor abnormality, such as a fluid overload or low potassium, didn't kill her. As far as I know, he never second-guessed his decision to intubate her.

Robert and I became friends, after a fashion. He didn't talk much. I never mentioned to him our conversation on the night Phyllis arrived. Phyllis's prolonged suffering wasn't his fault.

He saw Phyllis's message on the blackboard every day, but it was not addressed to him, and there was nothing he could do about the situation. His faith in her doctor and his belief that what was happening was best for her apparently remained unshaken.

Phyllis's treatment in the ICU cost thousands of dollars a day. Robert and Phyllis had reached the maximum on their insurance with her previous hospitalizations, and he was stuck with the bill for this one. Toward the end he told me he would have to sell the house in which he and Phyllis had raised their family. Not paying a hospital bill would never have occurred to him.

I finished my medicine rotation and said good-bye to Phyllis. A few days later, as I was sitting in the cafeteria for lunch, Dr. Hastings stopped by my table and said with great sadness, "I'm afraid we lost Mrs. Shattuck last night. She put up a great fight, but her cancer finally got her, and she passed on."

I moved on in my residency from Internal Medicine to Obstetrics, replacing care at the end of life with the miracle of birth. It wasn't until I began my career as an ER doc in rural Washington State that I was once again plunged into end-of-life issues and the lessons of Phyllis Shattuck began to resonate in my thinking.

I came to see that the problems in our society's approach to death are understandable and arise from the medical mandate to heal—a principle tempered by the fundamental admonition to, first, do no harm. In the face of miraculous technological advances in medicine, we have lost sight of how to avoid unnecessary suffering at the end of life.

REFLECTIONS

Dr. Hastings was a product of his training and conditioning. At the time of Phyllis's death, some twenty-five years ago, doctors had little or no training in dealing with death and dying. His training lacked any discussion about the natural process of death—how patients die, how medicine can contribute to their comfort as they die, how families are impacted by the death of a loved one—or what decisions would have to be made as the patient neared death.

About ten years earlier Dr. Elisabeth Kübler-Ross had published her landmark book, *On Death and Dying*, which broke ground by addressing these issues. Many medical students and residents encountered that book the first time they had to break bad news to a cancer patient, and they often recommended it to terminally ill patients and their families. However, few of the busy doctors-in-training I knew found time to read it themselves.

Although medical technology has advanced greatly since Phyllis's death, most doctors still graduate from medical school with basically no training in end-of-life situations. The average medical textbook still has fewer than twenty-five pages out of thousands on the subject of death and dying. And there is still little discussion in medical school of the effects of medical technology on people's lives.

Even when doctors do openly discuss these matters, patients and their families often unwittingly fail to hear. Our societal fear of death prevents productive discussion of end-of-life care. This book aims to vanquish that fear.

HOW THIS BOOK WILL HELP

By the time you finish reading this book you will have all the information you need to approach your Contract for Compassionate Care, which lets you choose what medical treatment you want or don't want at the end of your life. You'll learn about the contract by going through the decision-making process we call the Compassion Protocol.

The contract is a simple one-page form important to anyone at any stage of life. As you will see in the stories that follow, advance planning for end-of-life care is as crucial for healthy young people as it is for those who know they are at the end of life.

The Contract for Compassionate Care presents a new option that is omitted from most current Advance Directives: It gives you the option to choose a natural death. For example, Phyllis Shattuck could have chosen to receive Comfort Care Only (such as oxygen and antianxiety medication) instead of the interventions that painfully prolonged her life at a time when she was ready to die.

Choosing to die a natural death requires some serious decision making and rethinking of end-of-life options. It is an assumption in our society that all possible medical treatment will be used to keep us alive as long as possible. Breaking from that assumption, which many of us might choose to do, cannot be treated lightly.

The Compassion Protocol is a process that provides structure for your thinking as you face this difficult decision. It contains five simple steps for planning your end-of-life care. The first step educates you about the options you will have if you want to let a natural death occur. These options are simple medical treatment choices that reject the priority of keeping us alive as long as possible.

In the second step, we lead you through the decision-making process of choosing which option is right for you. In this step you also learn the importance of having a Health Care Decision

Maker whom you trust to implement your choices if you become mentally incapacitated.

The third step is all about communication. A major advantage of the Compassion Protocol is that it opens a dialogue between you and your family, friends, and health care professionals regarding your end-of-life care. This dialogue is all too often absent in our society.

In the fourth step, you will sign your Contract for Compassionate Care and formalize the choices you have made. It is important to note that the paperwork comes after the communication. This is because the paperwork will not work if the communication hasn't laid the foundation. By the end of step three, you and your Health Care Decision Maker will be on the same page. He or she should clearly understand what you want if you are unable to make your own decisions. In an age when the incidence of Alzheimer's dementia is rising rapidly this is critically important.

By the time you get to the fifth step you have done the hard work. All that is left is planning the kind of death you want.

Perhaps the Compassion Protocol's greatest strength is that it is communication based. One recent study found that 80 percent of designated Health Care Decision Makers have never discussed end-of-life treatment options with the family member who trusts them to make their choices. In completing the Compassion Protocol you can avoid this predicament by ensuring that all the important people in your life know what you want, and are prepared to carry out your choices.

Phyllis Shattuck provided Dr. Fitzpatrick with early and unforgettable lessons on what needed fixing in how we die.

LESSONS TO LEARN

Phyllis Shattuck's story introduces a key concept of the Compassion Protocol: the exit event. As we've discussed, an exit event is a naturally occurring illness that, if left untreated, will probably cause death. Pneumonia is a common potential exit event.

In the chronically ill or extreme elderly, weak chest wall muscles prevent deep breathing and coughing. Lung tissue that isn't fully expanded collects fluid, and the result is infection by bacteria—pneumonia.

Similarly, the chronically ill are often incontinent and are unable to fully empty their bladder of urine, predisposing them to urinary tract infections—another possible exit event.

Anyone who is bedridden is also at risk for damage to their skin, resulting in skin ulcers and infections.

Noninfectious potential exit events include cardiac events (arrhythmias or congestive heart failure), kidney failure, and, as in Phyllis's case, respiratory arrests. Simple dehydration also will cause death if untreated.

When Phyllis arrived in the ER gasping for breath, she was experiencing a potential exit event. If we had not treated her by putting her on a ventilator, she would have slipped into unconsciousness and died.

Phyllis had openly stated her desire to die at home as soon as possible, but her husband understandably could not stand to watch her suffer at home. Unfortunately, once she arrived at the hospital, she lost control of her own treatment. Instead of being made comfortable until she died, as she wanted, she was kept alive for six long, painful weeks.

People who have reached the point at which extending life equates with extending suffering need a way to say, like Phyllis Shattuck, "Enough. Just let me die." And our society and our medical system need a way to hear and respect patients' wishes under those circumstances.

Our Compassion Protocol was developed to enable patients in end-of-life situations to choose to take advantage of an exit event and die a natural death. It also allows young, healthy people to make proactive choices even when death seems like a distant event.

NEW NAME, OLD CONCEPT

Although discussion of exit events is new to most people, the concept was well understood by past generations. Before antibiotics were invented in 1943, doctors called pneumonia "the old man's friend" because it offered the very elderly a relatively quick and painless death, allowing them to avoid months or years of slow, painful decline.

Antibiotics have revolutionized medical care and greatly helped the sick and suffering. But these antibiotics and a host of other miraculous medical advances have also changed how we die. Death rarely comes suddenly anymore. It more often follows a long, slow decline into extreme old age marked by increasing frailty and debility, and sometimes dementia.

During that decline several possible exit events will occur. Each time, the patient will be taken to the Emergency Room and treated to cure the acute illness. Doctors and loving caretakers too frequently postpone death without adequate concern for the patient's quality of life or the amount of suffering that prolonging life will cause. If a person reaches the point that he or she no longer wants to continue that slow decline, that person has the option of requesting a natural death, quitting curative treatment, staying home with attention to comfort care, and dying sooner rather than later.

There are three groups of patients who, like Phyllis Shattuck, need a way to tell their doctors to withhold curative treatment and let them take advantage of their next possible exit event: the terminally ill, the extreme elderly whose quality of life has deteriorated intolerably, and patients who are living with dementia but who previously instructed their Health Care Decision Maker that they don't wish to live on in the fog of Alzheimer's. How each of these groups may benefit from increased choice and control at the end of life is discussed in detail in the chapters that follow.

CHAPTER TWO

YOUR RIGHT TO DIE

The phrase "Your right to die" can push many buttons. Let us state clearly: We are not talking about suicide, assisted suicide, doctor-assisted suicide, or any other political "hot potato."

This chapter is about the right of a mentally competent adult to refuse medical treatment even if to do so will result in death. By so doing, such a person has chosen to die a natural death sooner rather than later.

In fact, we contend that with the hope of achieving a natural death in this way through the Compassion Protocol, fewer people suffering the horrible pains of a terminal illness or chronic disease will seek the path of suicide, whether assisted or not.

This right to die has been established and clarified by the Supreme Court of the United States over the past eighteen years, most recently in the highly publicized Terri Schiavo case. This chapter examines the development of these laws as the legal foundation upon which the Compassion Protocol is built.

Twenty-five years ago Phyllis Shattuck's death greatly impacted Dr. Fitzpatrick. At about the same time, Karen Ann Quinlan's death became a landmark case in the Right to Die movement. A brief synopsis of Karen's story follows. Her story is treated comprehensively, with comments from many of those involved, in *The Good Death* by Marilyn Webb.

YOUR RIGHT TO DIE IS BORN:
THE CASE OF KAREN ANN QUINLAN

Karen was a healthy twenty-one-year-old woman who stopped breathing and entered a coma after a friend's birthday party. The cause of her coma remains uncertain, but it is known that she had two episodes of apnea—not breathing—before she arrived at the hospital. Each of these episodes lasted about fifteen minutes, long enough to cause irreparable brain damage.

In the Emergency Room at the local hospital, the doctor intubated her and attached her to a ventilator. While these measures kept Karen alive, the doctors conducted exhaustive tests to determine the cause of her coma.

At first everyone involved hoped that Karen would wake up, and everything possible was done to keep her body healthy. The ventilator breathed for her, forcing air into her lungs. She received the best nutritional support available via a tube placed through her nose into her stomach. Physical therapists worked to keep her limbs from permanently curling inward and her muscles and joints from freezing up. For three months her parents and sisters hoped and prayed for her recovery.

A Painful Decision

After four months her doctors and her family very reluctantly decided that there was no hope. Karen's parents had watched her body shrivel, despite the best care. Her doctors, including the best neurologists in the area, now classified her condition as a persistent vegetative state with no chance of recovery.

Her family slowly and painfully came to the difficult decision to end Karen's suffering and let her die by turning off the ventilator. They relayed this decision to Karen's doctor, who insisted on a consultation with hospital administrators before disconnecting the ventilator.

Karen was hospitalized at a Catholic hospital whose administration had never made this kind of decision before.

Two days later, at a meeting with hospital administrators, Karen's family was told that their wishes would not be honored. The Quinlans began a legal battle to have Karen removed from life support, and each step was covered extensively by the media.

A Clash of Values, a Philosophical Conflict

Aligned against the Quinlans was an impressive group of attorneys, including the New Jersey attorney general, representing the hospital and its doctors. They argued that disconnecting Karen's ventilator would amount to homicide.

To counter their claim, many of Karen's friends testified that she had directly and explicitly told them she would not want to be kept alive if she were in a coma with no chance of recovery.

The initial ruling on the case was in favor of the hospital administration. The judge's decision stated that Karen had no right to die, that her parents had no right to make medical decisions for her, and that the ventilator would stay.

THE RIGHT TO DIE—A FIRST STEP

Karen's parents appealed. In 1976, almost a year after Karen fell into her coma, the New Jersey Supreme Court ruled that Karen's father was her legal guardian and that his decisions regarding her care were legally binding. The court ordered Karen's doctor to disconnect her ventilator.

Over thirty years later this may seem obvious to most of us, but it was a revolutionary change at the time. Doctors were now legally allowed to take the active step of disconnecting life support equipment for hopeless cases after receiving permission from a parent or legal guardian.

In an ironic twist of fate, after Karen was disconnected from the ventilator, she began to breathe on her own—unaided by machines. She still received artificial nutrition by way of a feeding tube. Karen lived for nine more years, still in a persistent vegetative state, breathing on her own, and sustained by a feeding tube. She finally died from pneumonia in 1985.

Karen Quinlan's case was widely publicized, and each development was passionately debated across the nation. The Quinlan family's tragedy led President Jimmy Carter and the legislature to form a presidential commission whose report became the basis for state laws written to protect a patient's right to die.

THE SUPREME COURT WEIGHS IN: THE CASE OF NANCY CRUZAN

The Quinlan case was monumental, but the New Jersey Supreme Court's ruling applied only to the citizens of New Jersey. It took thirteen more years for the right to die to be established on a national level after the U.S. Supreme Court heard the case of Nancy Cruzan. For a more detailed look at this landmark case, see *Long Goodbye* by William H. Colby.

Nancy Cruzan was only twenty-five years old in January 1983 when she lost control of her car, was thrown into a ditch, and stopped breathing as a result of the impact. Although the ambulance paramedics got her breathing again, Nancy never regained consciousness.

Like Karen Ann Quinlan, Nancy was diagnosed as being in a persistent vegetative state. Doctors who examined Nancy and testified on her behalf estimated that she could live in a persistent vegetative state for another thirty years as long as she received nutrition through a feeding tube.

Feeling that their daughter's condition had placed her in a kind of limbo between life and death, her parents requested that the feeding tube be removed and that Nancy be allowed to die. The Missouri rehabilitation center where Nancy was being treated refused to honor the family's request.

A Missouri state court ruled in favor of the family's right to determine Nancy's treatment. The Missouri Supreme Court overruled the lower court judge, however, saying that the state's greater duty to preserve life outweighed any right the parents might have to refuse treatment for their daughter.

A HARD-AND-FAST RULING

In December 1989, thirteen years after the Quinlans' victory in the New Jersey Supreme Court, the Cruzan case became the first right-to-die case heard by the Supreme Court of the United States. In its decision the U.S. Supreme Court upheld the Missouri Supreme Court's position that not even the family could make choices for an incompetent patient. Only the patient could determine his or her treatment. If, however, family and friends could present evidence sufficient to meet a "heightened evidentiary standard," a court may order life support discontinued.

In the twenty years since the Cruzan case, the "heightened evidentiary standard" has been interpreted by some state courts to mean "clear and convincing evidence." Any evidentiary standard is at the mercy of its interpreters; nonetheless, we will refer to the clear and convincing evidence standard as it is possibly more accessible to the lay reader.

To accommodate the ruling of the U.S. Supreme Court, three of Nancy's friends came forward and related conversations with Nancy prior to the accident. In these conversations she expressed the conviction that she would never want to live if she fell into an irreversible coma. As a result, the State of Missouri withdrew its opposition, and the feeding tube was removed. Nancy Cruzan died shortly thereafter.

ONLY YOU CAN CHOOSE YOUR END-OF-LIFE CARE

The Cruzan case establishes the important rule that only you can make the decision to discontinue your life support. No one can choose for you. Moreover, you must clearly and convincingly tell your friends and family what your wishes are—or, better yet, put them in writing.

Note that according to this case and other similar legal opinions, no one can interfere with your clearly stated wishes for end-of-life care. Most of the laws and battles since Nancy Cruzan have been about *how* a person may clearly express such wishes or about the mess that occurs when a dying person has failed to clearly express his or her wishes while still able to do so.

ADVANCE DIRECTIVE FORMS: AN IMPERFECT SOLUTION

The decision in the Cruzan case means that if a patient has clearly and convincingly stated a desire not to be kept alive by life support, medical personnel are required to respect those wishes.

Advance Directive forms were developed to safeguard your right to die by allowing you to give clear and convincing instructions as to your wishes. These forms will be used to direct your end-of-life care if you are unable to make your own decisions.

Advance Directive is a catchall term used to designate any or all of the following forms:

1. **Living Will:** a legal document in which you state your wishes regarding the administration of life support if you are terminally ill or in a coma. It covers whether you want to be kept alive with a respirator or a feeding tube.

2. **Do Not Resuscitate (DNR) Order:** an instruction signed by your doctor that you do not want heroic measures used to resuscitate you, including CPR, if you stop breathing or your heart stops beating.

3. **Power of Attorney for Health Care:** a legal document in which you appoint a family member or friend as your Health Care Decision Maker. He or she will tell the doctors what your wishes are if you are mentally incapacitated, permanently unconscious, or in a coma.

4. **Physician Orders for Life-Sustaining Treatment, or POLST Form:** a contract between you and your doctor in which the doctor agrees to the care you will receive if you decide you are ready for death and no longer want curative care.*

Advance Directive forms are the legal documents you use to tell the world what you want done at the end of your life. Through-

---

*My experience is only with the Oregon POLST form, and all references to POLST refer to it. For information about the national task force working to make similar forms available in other states, go to www.POLST.org.

out the book we use the term *Advance Directive* to refer generally to any or all of these legal documents.

Federal law now requires health care facilities to discuss Advance Directive forms with patients when they are admitted to the hospital. Many elderly people in this country have signed these documents, which instruct their loved ones, their legal representative, and their doctor what measures they want taken or avoided when they are at the end of their lives. Information about access to Advance Directives is available on our Web site (www .compassionprotocol.com).

Doctors themselves began asking for Advance Directive forms in response to nightmare cases like Phyllis Shattuck's. Once someone is plugged into life support, as Phyllis was, it takes a deliberate act by someone to shut the machines off or to disconnect the patient. Doctors thus found themselves with the godlike power to give or take life.

To take a deliberate action to end a patient's life, doctors need the assurance that grieving family members won't turn around and charge them with murder, negligence, or malpractice. The wording and implementation of Advance Directive forms have been carefully legislated to protect both the patient and the doctor.

Phyllis Shattuck's death would have been very different had she lived in the era of Advance Directive forms. Someone as ill as Phyllis was during her last year, frequently in and out of the hospital, would likely have chosen to sign an Advance Directive instructing her doctor not to intubate her again. Dr. Hastings would have signed the directive along with Phyllis and would have been totally familiar with its instructions and Phyllis's wishes.

When Phyllis's husband, Robert, called Dr. Hastings because Phyllis was painfully uncomfortable at home, the doctor would still have told him to bring her to the hospital. But rather than being intubated, the hospital staff would have kept Phyllis comfortable until she died.

The Advance Directive form is not a perfect solution. For example, Phyllis might still have been intubated if she arrived at the ER by herself, or if she hadn't been able to tell the doctor her wishes before slipping into a carbon dioxide narcosis, or if the Emergency Room doctor had to make a split-second decision and was unaware of her wishes.

However, with an Advance Directive, Phyllis or her legal representative would have been able to order the machine disconnected and the life support withdrawn. She would not have suffered for six excruciating weeks, and her husband would not have lost his home because of huge hospital bills.

For religious or other reasons, some doctors or treatment centers still refuse to take that active step and honor a patient's right to die. Dr. Hastings may well have been one of those doctors. But even if the doctor refuses to honor the patient's wishes, the Advance Directive allows family, friends, and caregivers to advocate for the patient and make sure that both the patient's wishes and the law are followed by the doctor and the treatment center.

THE ALL-IMPORTANT
TERMINAL ILLNESS DIAGNOSIS

It is very important to realize, however, that these Advance Directive documents generally apply only very narrowly: You must be in a coma or have been pronounced terminally ill by your doctor.

The definition of "terminally ill" has been much debated in the courts and among end-of-life caregivers. Phyllis Shattuck, with lung cancer that had destroyed her lungs, was clearly terminally ill. But what about a patient with congestive heart failure who has also been in and out of the hospital for a year, and in addition, on and off ventilators?

What of the patient with Alzheimer's dementia who has been in a nursing home for six years and can no longer feed himself, or who has not moved on his own or interacted with his environment for two years? According to current medical practice, he is not considered terminally ill. His body is not ill at all. If he chokes on his dinner and goes into respiratory arrest, does his Living Will with its Do Not Resuscitate order allow his caregiver to let him die in accordance with his wishes? The current answer is usually no. His caregiver will call 911, and he will be resuscitated and transported to the Emergency Room.

Most people living in nursing homes are neither in a coma nor considered terminally ill. Under current practices, unless you have been declared terminally ill, the nursing home staff will probably send you to the ER for treatment the next time you have a fever, a cough, or some other reversible illness. They will send you again and again even if that is not what you want, unless your doctor declares you terminally ill. As you will see, the Compassion Protocol is specifically designed to remedy this dilemma.

Studies have shown that doctors are remarkably poor at predicting the remaining life span of patients with nonmalignant heart and lung disease. Some patients who have been designated terminally ill have lived for five years or more, with reasonable quality of life. Far more patients die before their doctors designate them as terminally ill. But who decides what it means to be terminally ill?

The courts have determined that to be considered terminally ill you must have less than six months to live. And although the courts have rendered this definition of terminal illness, doctors generally require that the patient's condition be "imminently fatal."

The requirement of a terminal illness diagnosis has been a sticking point in the crusade for more compassionate care at the end of life. Recently, some states have passed laws specifically stating that Advance Directives must be followed even without a diagnosis of terminal illness. Oregon has what are probably the most aggressive end-of-life patient protections. It has not only created the Physician Orders for Life-Sustaining Treatment, or POLST form, but Oregon's laws establishing patients' rights specifically state that a terminal illness diagnosis is not necessary to withhold curative care.

One would hope that the creation of such laws would herald a new approach to end-of-life care—an expansion of the patient's choice and control at the end of life. Sadly, change has been slow to come. As you will see in the coming chapters, it is difficult for the medical establishment to let go of the perceived duty to cure illness.

The Compassion Protocol consists of specific steps you can take now, while you are still in control of your mental faculties, to greatly increase the likelihood that your end-of-life wishes will be followed.

THE MORE THINGS CHANGE, THE MORE THEY STAY THE SAME: THE CASE OF TERRI SCHIAVO

Advance Directive forms continue to be critically important, as illustrated by the furor in the spring of 2005 over the case of Terri Schiavo in Florida. Terri had a heart attack in 1990 at the age of twenty-six and had been in a persistent vegetative state ever since. Because of her persistent vegetative state, her husband asked her caregivers to remove her feeding tube and let her die.

Terri's parents went to court to prevent Terri's feeding tube from being removed. They claimed that Terri still responded to their voices with movement, although doctors called these movements involuntary muscle activity. For Terri's family her apparent responses were reason enough to maintain her feeding tube.

The legal battle dragged on for years, and Terri's condition did not change. Terri's husband, Michael Schiavo, argued that Terri had always clearly expressed her desire never to be kept alive by machines or other artificial means.

Had Terri executed an Advance Directive that set forth this preference prior to her heart attack, we might not recognize her name today. In all probability there would have been no media coverage at all because her Advance Directive would have met the clear and convincing evidence standard set forth in the Cruzan case.

Private Tragedy, Political Grandstanding

Unfortunately, media coverage of the Schiavo case turned Terri Schiavo into a political football, creating additional pain and suffering for everyone involved. The case ground through the Florida courts for years, with husband Michael prevailing at key points.

Passions ran high, with Right to Die advocates arrayed against the Right to Life lobby. The case would take years to resolve and eventually involved both Congress and the U.S. Supreme Court, while Terri Schiavo lingered on in a persistent vegetative state, kept alive only by her feeding tube.

The end came for Terri amidst a highly publicized last-ditch effort by her family and their political supporters to advance their agenda. A confrontation between Right to Life activists and Florida troopers was narrowly averted when Florida Governor Jeb Bush finally decided to let the court's decision stand. Terri Schiavo died on March 31, 2005, thirteen days after her feeding tube was removed for the last time.

A Matter of National Debate

Many people felt passionately about the outcome of the case. Even the authors of this book disagreed. Dr. Fitzpatrick felt that Terri Schiavo's wishes, as stated to her husband, Michael, that she would not want to be kept alive artificially with severe brain damage, should have been honored—that Terri had a right to die. Attorney Fitzpatrick felt there was a legitimate question as to Terri's cognitive state, that she appeared to grunt in response to family greetings, and that the Court never adequately addressed the issue of whether a diagnosis of "minimally conscious" might be appropriate. Dr. Fitzpatrick felt there was no legitimate question as to Terri's cognitive state: Terri was clearly in a persistent vegetative state, and so her wishes should have been honored.

Remember, Terry Schiavo had no Advance Directive form. Had she signed that document—yes, even as a healthy young woman—it would have designated the person Terry trusted most with this decision, and that person would have had the legal right to enforce Terry's wishes. Terry's very public battle was a resounding call: Avoid putting your family through similar sorrow by completing your Advance Directive or Compassion Protocol even though you are young and healthy.

The public furor over this case illustrates the strong emotions surrounding the subject of death in our society. The authors' intense discussions over the Schiavo case, like those of many Americans, continue unabated. If nothing else, the Schiavo case points out the enormity of the emotional pain and suffering that can result from not having Advance Directive forms, regardless of one's age.

Phyllis Shattuck, Karen Quinlan, Nancy Cruzan, and Terri Schiavo typify two of the three different groups of people whom the Compassion Protocol is designed to serve. The first group, including Karen, Nancy, and Terri, comprises healthy people who suffer trauma or an unexpected medical catastrophe, and who can now be allowed to die when it is determined that there is no chance of their recovery. The second group is typified by terminally ill people like Phyllis who become ready to end their suffering by dying as comfortably as possible and who want to refuse artificial means to prolong their lives. The third group, the most controversial, is that of Alzheimer's patients who have chosen natural death while they are still sentient. This last group is discussed at length in chapter 5, Alzheimer's Dementia and the Compassion Protocol.

MOVING FORWARD: COMFORT CARE ONLY AND THE COMPASSION PROTOCOL

As the discussion above illustrates, there are many conditions that are not terminal but that create misery and suffering beyond what a human being should have to endure. We believe the solution to these problems lies in allowing people in extreme circumstances to choose to cease curative care, to receive comfort care for their symptoms, and to allow death to occur naturally. This is the heart of the Compassion Protocol. But first we must understand what it means to discontinue curative care and choose Comfort Care Only.

CEASING CURATIVE CARE

The right to die has been supported by legislation passed since the 1970s. Most states now protect a patient's wish to avoid aggressive medical intervention at the end of life.

But modern medicine can keep us alive far beyond what was previously considered a natural life span. As a result, there are four times as many nursing home beds in the country now as there were forty years ago.

For most of us, death will not come suddenly. Instead, it will approach slowly, by way of a gradual decline into chronic illness. We are likely to spend the last years of our lives slowly losing the things that make life worth living: first, the enjoyment of a vigorous life; next, our ability to socialize; and then, our ability to reason and even to care for ourselves. Eventually we may fall into a state of physical suffering, dependence, and isolation, locked in a process of decline from which death is the only escape. Or— possibly the worst fear of the boomer generation—we may fade slowly into the fog of Alzheimer's dementia, gradually losing reason and intellect in a healthy but mindless body.

The Compassion Protocol enables you to exercise your right to cease curative care. This is medical care that treats your illness—your possible life-ending exit event—and is aimed at restoring you to health. Curative care is the backbone of the medical system, and it keeps us alive and well.

But when your health declines and you reach the point that life is no longer preferable to death, you have the right to choose not to be kept alive with curative care. You have the option to choose Comfort Care Only instead and allow your next exit event to cause a natural death without interference.

CHOOSING COMFORT CARE ONLY

"Comfort care" is medical care that keeps you comfortable but makes no effort to treat an underlying disease. You have the right to choose to receive only comfort care instead of curative care. When you choose Comfort Care Only, the medical system will offer you medicines and support to keep you comfortable while your death approaches.

Comfort Care Only describes the role of the medical system and is not to be confused with palliative care. Comfort care specifically meets the medical needs of the dying, while palliative care addresses their physical, social, emotional, and medical needs.

Choosing Comfort Care Only means that you have decided you want to die a natural death. Instead of life-sustaining or life-prolonging treatment, you will receive only treatment that provides for your comfort and ease. Comfort Care Only patients have chosen to take advantage of the next exit event that comes along, allowing that occurrence to cause their death without interference.

Discussions of Comfort Care Only should not be limited to the elderly and the sick. The Compassion Protocol also allows young and healthy people to consider future circumstances in which they might like to limit medical treatment and to communicate their wishes to a Health Care Decision Maker.

What does that mean? It means you can choose not to be sent to the hospital if you develop an infection. You can choose not to receive IV fluids if you stop eating or become dehydrated. Usual medications, except those that provide comfort, may be stopped. If you are diabetic, insulin can be stopped. Most of the medications treating hypertension, congestive heart failure, or elevated cholesterol can be stopped. Medications for anxiety, insomnia, and especially for pain control will be continued.

An Important Distinction: Euthanasia and Doctor-Assisted Suicide

It is important to distinguish the choice of Comfort Care Only from active-assisted suicide or euthanasia. Patients choosing Comfort Care Only are not asking their doctors or family members to hasten or cause death by, for example, administering sedatives or other lethal medications. They are merely asking that those interventions administered to keep them alive in the past, whether routine medications or acute care of treatable illness, be withheld so that they may take advantage of their next naturally occurring opportunity to die.

The Compassion Protocol— a Better Solution

The Compassion Protocol tackles the persistent problem of the terminal illness diagnosis. We propose that the option of Comfort Care Only, which is currently available only to the terminally ill, should be extended to anyone who falls into one of our three groups: the sentient (or mentally competent) elderly, the terminally ill, and the demented who chose a timely natural death and filed their paperwork prior to the onset of dementia. The Compassion Protocol will help ensure that your choice of Comfort Care Only will actually be implemented in the rough and tumble world of modern health care.

Only someone who is ready to die will choose to restrict treatment to the administration of Comfort Care Only. Often, their Health Care Decision Maker will implement their choices for them because they are incapacitated from illness or age. Most patients choosing Comfort Care Only and executing a Contract for Compassionate Care (see chapter 9, Step Four: Do the Paperwork, and appendix A) will be at the end of a long battle against illness or will be living a life whose quality has deteriorated beyond repair.

A PERSONAL CHOICE

Our mother, now eighty-five years old, has watched many of her friends grow old and die. She can easily identify what she doesn't want to happen for her own death. She definitely doesn't want to live and die in a nursing home. "Shoot me before you put me in one of those, please," she says.

She doesn't want to be happily insane, unaware of her surroundings, with the mind of a two-year-old and needing the same care as an infant. She doesn't want to slowly starve to death in the grip of a cancer that eats painfully away at her body and her self-respect.

She signed typical Advance Directive forms in 1990 but knows these legal steps will not save her from her worst fear: losing her physical and mental control. In more serious moments our happy, life-affirming mom has made us promise that we will not let her live when her mind is gone or when she can't take care of herself or when a terminal illness is tormenting her body on a daily basis.

Many people share our mother's view of what they don't want for the end of their life. A lot of baby boomers vehemently voice their own preferences as they deal with the reality of having to place their parents in nursing homes. Advance Directive forms repeatedly fail in the task of saving us from the suffering of a slow, painful decline or from many years of wandering in the maze of Alzheimer's dementia.

The Compassion Protocol offers a person the opportunity to choose a natural death when he or she has arrived at the point at which life offers only continued suffering, loneliness, dependence, and sorrow. Read on to learn what measures you can take to retain control of your medical care and to ensure that you are allowed to die when you are ready.

WHO CAN USE THE COMPASSION PROTOCOL

The Compassion Protocol was designed to meet the needs of three groups of people: (1) the competent elderly (those who retain decision-making ability), (2) the terminally ill, and (3) the demented who empowered a Health Care Decision Maker prior to their decline.

As you will see, these three groups are carefully defined and detailed in scope. We never lose sight of the fact that the Compassion Protocol enlists family, friends, and the medical establishment to support and assist an individual's choice to refuse curative care and allow death to occur naturally, sooner rather than later.

The following three chapters focus on each of these three groups and how they can benefit from the increased choice and control at the end of life that the Compassion Protocol offers.

CHAPTER THREE

THE COMPETENT ELDERLY

Elderly people who retain their mental faculties often visit the Emergency Room over and over again. This phenomenon is so common that ER personnel invented the acronym LOLROGS, for Little Old Ladies Running Out of Gas. These are the extreme elderly—people in their eighties and nineties who are debilitated by a variety of illnesses. Most are women, since women generally live longer. Many are dependent on twenty-four-hour care to receive food, maintain their personal hygiene, and so on. They are not considered to be "terminally ill," but they are creeping slowly and inevitably toward death. Meanwhile, doctors keep them alive with long lists of medications and frequent trips to the Emergency Room. Possible exit events are treated and cured so that life can go on. But what if it is not a life worth living?

DR. FITZPATRICK TELLS
WILLA SIMPSON'S STORY

I was working in an ER serving the farming community of Oregon's Willamette Valley. Early one spring day an ambulance called to report the imminent arrival of a ninety-two-year-old female patient described as "coughing and unresponsive." It was a code one, meaning that the patient was not in extremis and the ambulance wasn't using lights and a siren. We recognized the pickup address as the local nursing home.

Nursing home patients soon become individuals to me, but my first impression is always of someone *old*. Male or female, large or small, awake or asleep, they share a frailty, a loss of strength, a diminution of spirit that seems to derive from living in a sterile institution. (Of course I don't meet the healthy ones in my line of work.)

The ambulance paramedics wheeled in a stretcher carrying a frail, elderly person named Willa Simpson. Willa was an average-size woman with some muscle still on her bones. She was awake and watched attentively as she was wheeled down the hallway. She smiled at me when her ambulance gurney paused briefly while the paramedics handed me her paperwork before she was wheeled into her room.

Willa's papers told me she had asthma, coronary artery disease, congestive heart failure, chronic atrial fibrillation, degenerative arthritis, and some ten other chronic illnesses. It may be difficult to believe, but typical nursing home patients have about fifteen chronic illnesses listed in their file for which they receive treatment.

I was able to determine that Willa had been living in the "full care" section of the nursing home for eight years. The nurse's note indicated that she had choked on her breakfast and had seemed to have difficulty breathing during the rest of the morning, with occasional coughing spells that left her exhausted and less responsive.

As I approached her bed, Willa looked quite comfortable. Her eyes were closed, but her body held an alert position, not the relaxation of sleep. She had been connected to a monitor, which showed a normal blood pressure, an irregular heartbeat of atrial fibrillation with a ventricular response well controlled at about 90 beats per minute, and an oxygen saturation of 94 percent, which is pretty good for her age. She had been placed on oxygen through a nasal cannula, delivering 3 liters of oxygen per minute.

JUST LEAVE ME ALONE— I'LL BE RIGHT BACK

She opened her eyes as I approached her bed and then smiled at me. When I bid her good morning and asked how she was feeling, she said, "Fine, thank you, and how are you today?"

I asked her if she knew the name of the place where she was, and she said, "Well, it's the hospital, isn't it? I've been here before, but it looked different then. Is this the Canton, Oregon, hospital?" With this response she passed her mental status exam; she not only knew the name of the hospital but also recognized the recent remodeling.

"Why are you here today?" I asked.

"I don't know. I guess I must be sick. Isn't that why they send a person to the hospital?" Her voice was strong, and her words and tone held more than a little annoyance.

I asked, "Your nurses thought you were having trouble breathing. Does your breathing seem okay to you now?"

She took a deep breath and exhaled fully; then she took another one—good breaths for someone her age, showing adequate chest wall motion and good air movement. She contemplated things for a moment after the second breath before telling me, "Yes, I think my breathing is fine."

"Did you have a bad cough or trouble with your breathing earlier this morning?" I continued. "Something must have happened to make them send you to the ER."

Willa closed her eyes then, laid her head back on the pillow, and seemed to be suddenly asleep. Her body was relaxed, her chin had sunk to her chest, her mouth fell open, and the hand that I was holding suddenly went flaccid. Her pulse was still strong beneath my fingers, and her chest rose and fell in a regular breathing pattern.

I squeezed her hand. No response. I shook her shoulder and called her name. No response. I gently pinched the skin on her arm, testing her response to pain. Her arm pulled away from me, and she batted at my hand. Her eyes opened, and she looked right at me and said, "I'm all right, honey. Just leave me alone for a moment. I'll be right back." With that her eyes closed, and she seemed to sleep again.

I pulled up a chair and sat down by her bed. I had a multitude of choices in my next action of "caring for" Willa. Most ERs have standing orders for any patient admitted with "shortness of breath" or "difficulty breathing," and the orders would be executed before the busy doctor saw the patient. In many hospitals, well before this conversation or instead of it, Willa would have had a chest X-ray, a blood gas, and other lab work done before she ever saw the doctor, but this was a small hospital with less automation and more time for doctor–patient interaction. (In addition, I am one of the small but persistent minority of ER doctors who insist on seeing the patient first and deciding what orders are appropriate for the individual even though it is "less efficient.")

My observation of Willa indicated that her tests would probably show acceptable values for her age, a little hypoxia on the blood gas, and an enlarged heart on the chest X-ray. I would probably order those tests eventually, but for the moment I was willing to take Willa's advice and leave her alone for a bit. I was definitely intrigued by her promise to "be right back."

It was only a few minutes before she moved again. Her hand on my side of the bed moved over the sheets, patting them. The rest of her body and her facial expression continued its slack, sleeplike unconsciousness. I put my hand under hers on the sheet, and she squeezed it tight. She held my hand in a strong grip for another minute before she began to talk.

"I'm so close, you know, and this morning I felt the closest I've ever felt." Her eyes remained closed, and her voice sounded slow and dreamlike, different from the matter-of-fact tone of our earlier conversation.

"Death is just half a step away from me," she continued, "and sometimes I feel that if I just hold my breath for a minute, I can get there. I was so close this morning, and the nurse started yelling at me and made me come back. I guess I scared her, but I thought maybe I could just slip over the edge and be gone."

Her hand let go of mine then, and she again looked asleep or unconscious. I put her hand down and stroked her arm a few times. Her skin was thin and as pliant as tissue.

I stood and said to her, "It's okay, Willa. You sleep as long as you like. I'll come to check on you again in a bit." I went to review her chart again, leaving her looking peaceful and comfortable.

I HAVE TO DECIDE WHAT TO DO

The front page of her nursing home chart had a big DNR stamp on it, for Do Not Resuscitate. This meant she had filled out an Advance Directive and did not want to be brought back to life in the event of cardiac arrest and did not want to be kept alive by machines.

The chart listed a son in Modesto, California, as Willa's next of kin. It was the middle of the afternoon now, so I thought he was unlikely to be home, but I called his number to at least leave a message. I asked the woman who answered if I could speak to Martin Simpson. I told her I was calling from Oregon about his mother, Willa Simpson. She told me that Martin had died six months ago. She introduced herself as Barbara Simpson, Martin's wife and Willa's daughter-in-law. She said she knew her mother-in-law well and asked if she could help me.

I asked her when she had last seen Willa. "It's been about three years, just before Martin got sick the last time." She explained that Martin used to talk to his mother almost once a week, and she had tried to keep up with it after his death. However, she and Willa hadn't talked for a month. Was Willa okay?

"She seems fine," I replied. "She had a little trouble breathing this morning, but she's okay now. She indicated to me, though, that she seems to want to die. I wondered if she has ever talked to you about dying."

"Oh, good grief, yes. She talks about it all the time. Ever since her husband died and she had to move to the home, she's been telling everyone that she never wanted to live so long and really wishes death would hurry on up." Barbara told me Willa didn't want to go into the nursing home, but she eventually adjusted and seemed to be pretty happy there. "Why?" she asked, her voice tight with worry. "Do you think she's critically ill?"

"No, I actually think she's fine. She had some coughing spells this morning, and she's drifting a bit mentally, but she comes back and seems fine." I explained that her paperwork from the nursing home still listed Martin as her next of kin. "Does she have any other family around here?"

Barbara said that Martin was an only child. Willa and her husband, Merle, had some neighbor friends, but they had all passed away. Martin and Barbara's visit three years ago was probably the last time Willa had any visitors. Barbara didn't know who would be Willa's next of kin now. "Can't you ask her?" she wondered. "She seemed just fine the last time I talked to her, about a month ago. Is she unconscious?"

"No, she's awake. I'll talk with her some more. She must know Martin's dead, right?"

"Oh, yes, of course. She's not crazy or demented, at least not normally. She was as sharp as a tack the last time I talked to her."

More About How Willa Is "Ready to Move On"

I asked Barbara if she could tell me more about Willa's wanting to die. Had she been depressed or in a lot of pain?

"I don't think so. I think she's just tired of living. She has been just withering away for years. She barely gets out of bed anymore, she can't walk without assistance, and she can't read any longer. All she can do is watch TV, and she never much liked it. She doesn't complain much. It's not as if she always talks about how sick she is. She just says she's tired and ready to move on. That's what she calls it, moving on.

"She told me once that death is the only adventure left to her and that it has to be more interesting than her current life. And she looks forward to being reunited with her husband and Martin. She's a good Christian woman and knows she'll go to heaven."

We talked a little more, and I promised to call Barbara back or have Willa call her after we knew what was going on. I checked on my patient again. Willa was still "asleep," smiling faintly. Her breathing wasn't labored, and her vital signs were stable. I decided not to order any tests for now and wait to talk to her when she "came back."

Support from a Sympathetic Colleague

Willa's primary care doctor was a friend of mine, Dr. Jack Street. I had the nurse page him, and I told him about Willa. He agreed with my plan to just wait for now and not order the usual tests, since I thought there was really nothing wrong with her.

For the next few hours I checked on her often, as did the nurses. We didn't bother her except to talk quietly to her now and then, and she remained unresponsive to us, apparently asleep. The blood pressure cuff squeezed her arm every thirty minutes, but she was otherwise undisturbed. If she woke up during that time, we missed it.

After four hours I had the nurse order a dinner for her. I took it in and put it on a tray by Willa's bed. I told her it was there and what was on it, and I invited her to eat if she felt like it.

I checked her abdomen and could feel a very full bladder above her pubic bone. I told her, "Willa, I know your bladder is full. Would you like a bedpan? Or we can get you up to go to the bathroom whenever you want. Are you ready now?" No response.

The next time I checked on her, she had emptied her bladder on the bed. I had the nurse change her linens and put a diaper on her. She remained flaccid throughout the procedure, apparently not even noticing what we were doing. Her dinner was untouched.

I had let this go on long enough and needed to make a decision about her disposition. She couldn't stay in the ER indefinitely, and I was starting to think that if I left it up to her, she just might "sleep" indefinitely.

Willa would either have to go back to the nursing home or be admitted by her primary care doctor. I called Dr. Street again and filled him in on the past six hours.

"So do you think she's asleep?" he asked. "Or unconscious? Or what?"

"I think she's just pretending to sleep and doing a very good job of it. I think she'll probably open her eyes and talk to us at some point, but I don't know when. The fact that she wet the bed rather than wake up would seem to indicate she's pretty seriously tuned out. She must have tried this at the nursing home before. What do they do?"

"They've told me that sometimes they have to force her to eat," he replied, and he explained that Willa told him they actually force her jaw open to make her eat and drink. A few years ago they had some major battles over it, but he thought things had been going better lately. He hadn't heard anything about her from the nurses recently and was due to see her for her six-month checkup soon.

I said, "I can send her back to the nursing home, but I don't think they'll be happy with her acting this way. What will they do to her if she tries to stay asleep? She sure seems intent on staying asleep as long as we'll let her."

We discussed our options. Jack could admit her with a diagnosis of "altered mental status." In order to do that, she would have to have all the lab tests and probably a head CT as well, and he wasn't sure what that would accomplish. He asked me what I thought she wanted.

Is "Comfort Care Only" an Option for Willa?

I told him I thought she wanted to die. We hadn't talked very much before she shut down, but that was certainly my impression— that she just wanted to slip off into a coma and into death. She might have wanted to do that for a long time. I asked, "Can we let her do that?"

I mentioned the end-of-life protocol that Oregon had recently adopted, called the Physician Orders for Life-Sustaining Treatment, or POLST. In appropriate end-of-life situations, POLST allows patients to choose to stop curative care—treatments intended to cure their health problems and prolong their lives. Instead of curative care, patients can use the POLST form to receive only comfort care—treatment designed to keep them comfortable without concern for prolonging life. Could POLST be used for Willa Simpson?

Jack was intrigued and agreed to come in to see Willa for himself and help me decide what to do with her. The ER was busy now, and I didn't see him arrive. When the nurse told me that Jack was there, I found him sitting by Willa's bed, talking to her. He was saying, "We need to talk, Willa. I know you can hear me. Just open your eyes." I said hello to her, as I had been doing all day, and took her hand.

Jack continued, "You know, Willa, you're really presenting Dr. Fitzpatrick and me with quite a problem. We can't just let you sleep here in the ER forever. We have to send you back to the nursing home. I can make things very different for you there and have them leave you alone as we have here, but first we need to talk."

No response. Jack said, "We're going to examine you now, Willa." He grabbed her other arm and gently tugged. "Sit up for us."

She remained a dead weight, so he and I pulled her to a sitting position. Her back stayed straight, and she held up her head. If she were unconscious, her head would have rolled on her neck, and her back would have curved when we pulled on her arms. We listened to her lungs, laid her back down, checked her heart and her belly, and checked her reflexes. Then Jack took out his penlight to check her pupils.

He pulled back her eyelids, and she looked him right in the eye. He was startled and let go of her eyelids. She held his gaze for a few moments before closing her eyes again. Then she said, "I don't know what there is to talk about. I've been telling you for years that I want to die." It sounded like a gentle remonstrance to a recalcitrant toddler.

We Decide to "Just Leave Her Alone"

Willa added, "I just wish everybody would leave me alone so I could drift forever. It's so peaceful here. I probably wouldn't even notice if I died, except that then I wouldn't have to deal with those mean nurses anymore. You'd better just let me die now. You promised you would."

Her eyes were closed again. Jack said, "Okay, Willa, but first you have to sign some papers to make it legal for me to do that. I'll help you, but you have to help me first. Will you?"

After a few moments she took a deep breath, opened her eyes, and said, "Okay, let's do it. What do we have to do?" She was the most awake and alert I had seen her, and she looked quite happy.

I left them to return to my busy ER. Jack had her sign an

Oregon POLST form, requesting Comfort Care Only. She elected to receive no antibiotics and no feeding tube or intravenous fluids. She would not ever again be sent to the Emergency Room unless she developed pain that required comfort measures available only at the hospital. This is as far as the Oregon POLST form goes.

A FORERUNNER OF THE COMPASSION PROTOCOL IS BORN

Jack also wrote an additional order for the nursing home to discontinue all her routine medications for her diabetes, her blood pressure, and her heart rhythm. She would still be offered medicines for pain, for anxiety, and for sleeplessness.

But Willa really wanted to stop receiving nutrition and liquids. Jack wasn't sure he could do this for her. He wrote an order stating that she was to be offered liquids to drink three times daily, but she would not be forced to drink anything. The nurses were instructed not to wake her up if she was sleeping.

She agreed to wear a diaper, though Jack said she fought that. She didn't want a diaper, but she was sure she didn't want to get up to urinate, either, and she didn't want a catheter permanently in her bladder. Jack had to convince her that she had to choose one of those three conditions, or else the nurses would choose for her—and he was sure she didn't want that.

Jack talked to the administrator at the nursing home. He was required to diagnose Willa as "terminal" before the home would comply with the Comfort Care Only orders. This required a second doctor to corroborate the diagnosis, and I did. Jack and I had few qualms about helping Willa achieve a death that she had been wanting for some time now.

WILLA GRADUALLY SAYS GOOD-BYE

During the next few days I visited Willa at the nursing home. She would wake up when I said her name, and we had long, pleasant conversations. She talked about her life, her husband, Merle, her son, and the farm where she grew up. She remained fully aware of what she was doing and was comfortable with her decision. Her Methodist minister visited her regularly. She said, "He told me what I'm doing is okay with God, but I already knew that. He's a nice man, and I enjoy his visits, but I can talk to God in my prayers without any help. We're okay, God and I."

At the end of each visit I asked her if she would like something to drink. She would smile and say, "No, thanks." On the third day she was noticeably weaker but still quite alert.

Willa talked to me for the last time on the fifth day, after which she slid quietly into a dehydration coma. Her heartbeat became steadily weaker, and she died on the tenth day after her visit to the Emergency Room.

LEARNING FROM WILLA

When I visited Willa in the nursing home during those ten days, I wondered how many other residents might have wanted to join her but didn't know how. I thought about all the frail, lonely, elderly people who had said to me in the ER, "Please let me die."

I had never felt empowered to let them die or to offer them the choice of nontreatment for whatever condition brought them to the ER. Directive forms such as Oregon's POLST could help them if they were diagnosed as terminally ill. But what of the typical Willas that fill the beds in a nursing home? What of the rapidly growing number of patients with advanced dementia who routinely receive curative treatment of possible exit events so that they can continue leading a life they might have preferred to leave? I came to believe we needed a new approach that could be offered to people at the end of a life that was no longer worth living.

Dr. Street and I were able to help Willa using legal tools that had already been developed. Oregon's POLST form allowed Willa to refuse curative care and to choose Comfort Care Only. Because we declared her "terminally ill," she was not forced to eat or drink and was not sent to the hospital when she became dehydrated.

THE COMPASSION PROTOCOL INCREASES CHOICE AND CONTROL AT THE END OF LIFE

The Compassion Protocol contains a more muscular version of the POLST form. The Compassion Protocol specifically does not require a diagnosis of terminal illness. Step Four of the protocol takes you through the Contract for Compassionate Care (see

appendix A) that allows patients to stop their maintenance medications and even stop receiving nutrition and hydration if they
so desire. Under appropriate circumstances our Compassion
Protocol allows patients like Willa to decide they are ready to die
and then slip gently into natural death.

THE COMPASSION PROTOCOL AND
THE COMPETENT ELDERLY

Willa Simpson typifies one group of people who can benefit from
the Compassion Protocol—the competent elderly. These are people who are mentally alert, oriented, and capable of making informed decisions but who live in a body that no longer tolerably
accommodates them.

How can someone be mentally alert and aware but not want
to live? Their bodies may be racked by pain from severe arthritis
or osteoporosis such that they can no longer even move in bed
without excruciating pain. They may have severe congestive heart
failure or advanced lung disease that makes the effort of breathing overwhelming, denies them comfortable sleep, and renders
even mild exertion impossible. In addition to enduring intolerable physical suffering, they may be stuck in a nursing home bed,
separated from their family and friends, and with no enjoyment
left in life.

For elderly people in such circumstances, life is no longer a
precious gift to fight for at any cost. Surviving for a few more
days, weeks, or months will add nothing to the sum of their lives
except more suffering and pain.

Because the legal standard for a "terminally ill" diagnosis is generally a life expectancy of less than six months, doctors rarely consider mentally competent extreme elderly patients to be terminally ill just because of their advanced age and debility. Neither the patients nor their doctors can be sure if they will live another few days, weeks, months, or even years. In fact, studies have shown that by the time doctors feel comfortable diagnosing this group as "terminally ill," they have less than ten days to live.

But the competent extreme elderly share a very serious reality with cancer patients who are easily identified as terminally ill. They all know that their lives will not become more comfortable or productive. Rather, they will decline in mind and body slowly and steadily while enduring increasing pain and suffering until death finally brings release.

The competent extreme elderly who are living in bodies worn beyond repair and are kept alive by a large assortment of daily medications and frequent trips to the hospital have the same rights as cancer patients to say, "Enough. Just let me die."

And when they reach the point of preferring death to life, they may use the Compassion Protocol to insist on being allowed to die a natural death by taking advantage of their next possible exit event. The next time their health is challenged, they will not be sent to the hospital for evaluation and treatment. Rather, they will remain at home or in their nursing home bed, receiving only the treatment they choose with the addition of medical comfort measures to ease suffering or discomfort. (Hospice programs are often already available to provide comfort measures for home deaths for those who can obtain a diagnosis of terminally ill. For more information see chapter 11, Hospice and the Compassion Protocol.)

Applying the Compassion Protocol to the competent elderly is not a radical change—it is, in fact, conservative in the best sense of the word. It conserves the natural death process that has worked for thousands of years to provide a timely death at the end of life. For elderly persons who feel they are ready to cease life's struggle, it allows death to come as a merciful release sooner rather than later.

CHAPTER FOUR

THE TERMINALLY ILL

The second group who can benefit from the Compassion Protocol are persons with a terminal illness. Does this sound simple, even self-evident? The designation of "terminal" is of paramount importance under current practices because it marks the point at which a patient may begin to receive Comfort Care Only.

Given the legal battles waged over the issues of life and death, it is not surprising that the courts have stepped in to define "terminally ill." The definition applies to those cases in which the patient has less than six months to live, as determined by two separate doctors.

Practically speaking, doctors err on the conservative side when making this diagnosis. People are often in the last days or weeks of life before they are deemed "terminal." In one study, most patients died within two weeks of being designated as "terminally ill." As patients become more proactive in managing end-of-life care, they may have to insist that doctors more accurately estimate when a person is actually terminal.

Many terminally ill patients reach a point where the pain

and suffering of illness make life no longer worth living. With no possibility of recovery or improvement, they face the certainty that things will only get worse. If you have seen someone die of cancer, you can probably imagine arriving at this point.

A patient may have fought cancer for years, undergoing the discomfort of chemotherapy and the pain of radiation treatment over and over until no possibility exists of again achieving remission. The cancer has overwhelmed the body's defenses and caused increasing levels of pain, weakness, and the inability to function at a tolerable level of comfort. The patient has been told by a doctor that nothing else can be done to treat the cancer and that the cancer will only get worse until death finally comes.

The following is a real-life story of one woman's suffering with end-stage cancer and how she and her family dealt with her approaching death.

DR. FITZPATRICK TELLS
MELISSA BLACKBURN'S STORY

Although Melissa Blackburn had never smoked a cigarette in her life, she died of metastatic lung cancer at the age of thirty-eight. She left behind a husband, Ron, and two children: Mandy, age twelve, and Jennifer, age fourteen.

I met the Blackburns in the Emergency Room on the last day of Melissa's life. With the help of hospice, friends, and other family members, the Blackburns had worked as a family to prepare emotionally and psychologically for Melissa's death. They had arrived together at the acceptance phase and planned to share Melissa's quiet passing at home. Despite their preparations and plans, events conspired to give them a difficult death.

Melissa had been a very active woman. She was a full-time wife and mother who hadn't worked since the birth of her first daughter. She made a full-time job out of being a soccer mom, a good cook, and a good wife. When Ron and his daughters talked about their life before her illness, Melissa sounded like a throwback to the 1950s, a Mrs. Cleaver mom. When Melissa noticed a little less energy one winter, she just pushed herself a little harder and ignored it.

Melissa's cancer was in an advanced stage when it was diagnosed. She didn't really feel ill before the diagnosis, although in retrospect she realized that she was getting short of breath with less exertion than usual for her and had less than her usual energy. She had always maintained an ideal weight with little effort, and she didn't really notice the five pounds she had lost over the course of the winter.

When she developed a pain in the right side of her chest, in the back just below her shoulder blade, she thought it was a pulled muscle; she took some Advil and did her best to ignore it. Instead of going away, it got steadily worse, but it was still three months before she went to her doctor about it.

Her doctor must have known her well, at least well enough to know that she would not be there with an insignificant complaint, because he ordered a chest X-ray on the first visit. Melissa had a wedge-shaped infiltrate in the posterior right lung—a shadow in the lung stretching from the center of the chest to the chest wall, meeting the chest wall right at the site of her pain. As soon as he saw the X-ray, her doctor ordered a CT scan, which confirmed that this was probably a bronchogenic carcinoma, a cancer usually seen in smokers. A biopsy made the final confirmation.

This had been two years earlier. Melissa had surgery to remove the tumor and opted for the most aggressive chemotherapy and radiation she was offered in hopes of completely obliterating the malignancy. She achieved a brief remission, recovering from her treatment and resuming the life of an active, fully engaged mom for a brief six months before the cancer showed up again in several spots in her lung and in her bones.

The family knew that the chance of a cure became just about zero after the metastases showed up. Ron, Mandy, and Jennifer began to think about life without Melissa, even as more chemotherapy was begun.

Two months before I met Melissa, she had a seizure and metastases were found in her brain and her liver. She was put on antiseizure medication and had radiation to the metastases in the brain to try to shrink them. She continued to have chemotherapy as much as her body could tolerate—no longer in hopes of a cure but in an effort to buy her as many extra weeks or months with her family as possible. The family began to plan for her death, and hospice became involved in her care.

Melissa took to her bed very reluctantly, but inevitably she became unable to care for her family or even herself as her very aggressive cancer consumed all her energy. A sister, Mary, moved in with the family so that Ron could continue his job as an accountant, and hospice provided a nurse who visited three times weekly. Melissa needed more and more pain medication. (Bone pain from metastatic disease is among the most painful conditions we know.) Hospice also made counselors available for Mandy and Jennifer; they could visit with the counselors as often as they wanted. The family drew close together and prepared for the end.

Melissa knew she wanted to die at home. One month before I met her, she signed Oregon's POLST form, asking to be allowed a quiet death at home with no more visits to the hospital or her doctor's office. Her daughters knew her wishes and were able to talk with the hospice counselor about their mom's death.

Melissa continued to support her body's nutritional needs as much as she could, taking Ensure and other nutritional liquids regularly, although eating solid foods now increased her discomfort considerably. She spent her days in bed, visiting with her family and sleeping, finding what comfort she could in increasing doses of narcotics and sedatives, and increasingly longing for the end to come.

THE BEST-LAID PLANS

It was certainly not Melissa's intent to go to the ER to die. When it happened, Mary had been with her most of the day but went out to do some shopping and was not there when Mandy and Jennifer got home from school. Mary was half an hour from home when she received a panicked call from Jennifer on her cell phone: Melissa had started to seize; she was turning purple, and there was blood pouring out of her nose and mouth. What should they do? Unable to imagine her two nieces being home alone as their mother died, Mary told Jennifer to call 911.

The ambulance was called out to the home of "a thirty-eight-year-old female with a seizure in progress." Two sobbing and incoherent teenagers greeted the paramedics and led them to Melissa, who was in the throes of a grand mal seizure. They could tell Melissa was near death by her emaciated form and the obvious sick-room environment. The girls said nothing about Melissa's POLST form or her wish to die at home, however, so the paramedics did everything they could to keep Melissa alive.

They were unable to protect Melissa's airway because she had bitten nearly through her tongue, and the heavy bleeding was filling her mouth. She had nearly choked to death on her own blood. If the ambulance had arrived five minutes later, Melissa's suffering would have been ended by this exit event. Instead, the paramedics paralyzed her and intubated her, started an IV, gave her 5 milligrams of Valium for the seizure, and transported her to the ER.

The paramedics called me twice during the ten-minute run to the hospital. The paralytic medication had worn off, and Melissa resumed seizing. This meant that although her seizure appeared to stop when her muscles were paralyzed, her brain continued to seize, so when the drug wore off, she resumed the tonic-clonic seizure activity.

I told them to give her another 10 milligrams of Valium because they had no other antiseizure medications with them. Fifteen milligrams of Valium was a lot, potentially enough to stop

Melissa's breathing, but the paramedics were already breathing for her using a bag attached to the endotracheal tube.

They called a second time to say Melissa was still seizing. To keep her safe during transport, I had them paralyze her again.

Dr. Fitzpatrick Faces Another Difficult Decision

Just after the second call from the paramedics, I received a call from Mary, Melissa's sister. She had arrived home just as the ambulance was pulling out with Melissa and called me as soon as she was able to calm the girls down.

Mary told me that Melissa had end-stage lung cancer and a POLST form requesting Comfort Care Only, and she told me briefly what had happened and why Melissa was on her way to the hospital. She asked me to make Melissa as comfortable as possible and said she, Ron, and the girls would be there soon. I told her to be sure to bring the POLST form with her.

I was just hanging up when the ambulance arrived as code four, with lights and sirens. The paramedics moved very quickly to get Melissa onto a stretcher and release her to us. The continued seizure, her apnea, and especially her youth combined to make them very uncomfortable. The paramedics continued to support her breathing through the tube in her lungs while the nurses connected her to the cardiac monitor and blood pressure cuff.

The second dose of paralytic medicine was starting to wear off, and Melissa had some movement back, just enough to tell me that she was still seizing. She was starting to breathe on her own through the endotracheal tube.

Without the intervening call from Mary and the additional history about Melissa's condition and her POLST form, I would immediately have treated her for status epilepticus—a seizure that continues longer than thirty minutes and doesn't respond to antiseizure medications. Curative treatment for status epilepticus involves first trying some lorazepam, a close relative of Valium that is slightly more effective against seizures. If that didn't work, she would get a loading dose of Dilantin as quickly as it could be given, and if that didn't work, she would get phenobarbital.

Instead of proceeding immediately with curative care, I first had to consider what the patient and her family would want me to do. Yes, take the tube out of her lungs even if it meant that she might die. I felt I couldn't legally and safely do this, however, until the family arrived with the POLST form.

In the meantime, I decided that stopping the seizures would be considered a comfort measure. I ordered the lorazepam and began to address the bleeding in Melissa's mouth so that she would have a chance to breathe on her own when I removed the tube.

But I couldn't see into her mouth. With the resumed seizure activity, her jaw was tightly clenched around the bite block on the tube, offering me no chance of finding and fixing the laceration of her tongue.

A suction tube placed next to the breathing tube by the paramedics continued to return a significant amount of bright red blood, indicating that Melissa was still actively bleeding too much to breathe on her own if the tube were removed. I would have to paralyze her again to fix the laceration or just pull the tube, knowing that she would drown in her own blood and die quickly.

The first dose of lorazepam did nothing to the seizure activity, and I ordered a second dose after five minutes. Melissa had been in the ER less than ten minutes, and until her family arrived, I decided to do nothing else except continue to attempt to end her seizures.

She continued to seize and received a third dose of lorazepam five minutes after the second. I asked the nurse to start the Dilantin drip, a strong antiseizure medication. This time I paralyzed her with a long-acting agent to stop the seizures and make it possible to ventilate her and repair her tongue laceration. Once she was immobilized, the respiratory therapist hooked her up to a ventilator, which delivered oxygen to her lungs.

A WELL-PREPARED FAMILY DEALS WITH THE UNEXPECTED

Mary and the girls arrived. Jennifer and Mandy were crying but calm, holding on to each other. They looked very frightened. As I walked up to them, Mandy, the youngest, said, "Is Mom dead?"

I told her that her mom was still alive but unconscious, and she was alive only because we were breathing for her through a tube into her lungs.

"We shouldn't have called you," said Jennifer. "I know Mom wanted to stay home, but it was so awful, we just panicked. Now that she's here, can't we just take her home before Dad gets here?"

I told her that her mom was still seizing and that we would

try to stop the seizure so she could go home. They wanted to see Melissa, but I asked them to wait until their father arrived.

Mary said she thought Ron would be there any minute. She gave me the bright pink POLST form requesting Comfort Care Only, and I left them to return to my patient.

The Dilantin was still infusing, and Melissa was still seizing. She lay still, her body relaxed by the paralytic. Only her eyes danced, moving rhythmically back and forth, showing that her brain was still firing its epileptic message. Her blood pressure was sky high, which is the case when anyone seizes, and the cardiac monitor showed a regular fast heartbeat.

Melissa's husband, Ron, arrived just a few minutes later. He ran into the ER yelling, "Where's Melissa Blackburn? Where's my wife?"

When I approached him and introduced myself, he gripped my arm painfully tight and demanded to see his wife. I took him to her, and he went right to the head of the bed and kissed her on the forehead. He had tears on his cheeks when he looked up at me. All he said to me was "Can I take her home now?"

I told him that she couldn't breathe on her own without the tube, and that if I took the tube out, she wouldn't live long enough to get home. He told me she never should have been brought to the hospital; she should have died at home. He told me to take the tube out and let her die.

"Your daughters and Mary are here," I told him. "They had a frightening time at home with her. She looks fine now with the seizure mostly controlled, but seeing someone you love have a seizure is a horrible thing. It's just not pretty. Can we let them see her and say good-bye first?"

He said, "God, I wish they hadn't called you. I wish we were all at home as we had planned."

"But that isn't what happened," I said. "You can't do anything more for Melissa, but your daughters need you right now. They will remember that seizure for the rest of their lives. You don't want it to be their last memory of their mother, and you don't want to make them feel guilty for doing what they did. Why don't I go get them and let you all have your last minutes with Melissa together here? We'll give you as much privacy as you need and as much time as you need. We'll take the tube out when you're all ready."

Ron and I both turned to look at Melissa. She was draped in a sheet to her neck. Her emaciated head was resting on its side with the endotracheal tube and suction catheter coming out of her mouth. Her eyes were closed. She might have been asleep but for the tubes. She looked peaceful. The respirator puffed quietly, and the cardiac monitor beeped its rhythm.

I brought Mandy and Jennifer in and left the four of them together. I peeked in after about five minutes. Ron had an arm around each daughter. Mandy stroked her mother's bald head, and Jennifer held her mother's hand. I wondered what I could do to ease the pain this day had brought. I could do nothing of importance for Melissa.

WHEN DEATH IS MESSY AND DOESN'T COOPERATE

Death stands as a barrier between the presence of someone we love and memories of that person. No matter how much preparation a family does for an untimely death like this, the actual moment of death must be endured and survived. If it is an awful moment, it can block loving memories of the deceased for months or years. When the mind recalls the mother or wife, the first images are of the horrible moment of death. It may be years before the mind can set aside those images and explore all the wonderful memories of the good times when health and happiness were abundant. I didn't want that for Melissa's daughters.

After another ten minutes I joined the family on the other side of Melissa's bed and asked, "Did you ever talk with Melissa about what the moment of her death would be like?"

Mandy answered without looking up at me, "She said she wanted us all to be together while she just drifted off to sleep. She always joked that it would probably be really messy . . ." Mandy started to sob and buried her head in her father's chest.

I told her that death was often like that, messy, like her Mom biting her tongue and bleeding a lot. I told her that I had seen a lot of people die, and very few of them had the comfortable, quiet death that Melissa wanted. What I didn't tell them was that no matter how their mother spent her last moments, the hard work of living without her would still be overwhelming to her daughters.

"I'd like to fix her tongue so the bleeding stops. Then we'll take that tube out when we have the mess under control. Is that okay with you?"

Ron seemed not to hear any of this. He hadn't looked up at me. Jennifer asked if it would hurt her mom. I told her no, that she wouldn't feel anything. They could stay and watch if they wanted.

An hour had passed since the last dose of paralytic. I could see the beginnings of muscle fasciculations that meant Melissa would soon be able to breathe on her own. It took me only a few minutes, with the family silently watching, to put enough stitches in her tongue to stop the bleeding. After I finished, Jennifer asked, "What happens next?"

"In about ten minutes I'll take the tube out of her lungs and let her breathe on her own, and you can take her home."

Ron looked up then. His eyes were angry, and his tone was gruff. "I thought you said she wouldn't live long enough to get home."

"Without the stitches she couldn't breathe because of the blood. I couldn't take the tube out until the stitches were in. Now she won't choke to death, but she's still having a seizure. None of the medications have been able to stop her seizure. There's one other medication I could give her that might work."

Mandy asked, "If she's still seizing, will she maybe bite her tongue again?" I could see in her frightened eyes the memory of her mother shaking and jerking, with blood pouring out of her mouth.

"No, she won't seize hard like that again because of the medications. She'll be just like she is now, apparently asleep. We can have the hospice nurse meet you at home to make sure her seizures don't get bad again. I don't think she'll wake up and talk to you again. She'll probably just stay like this until she quietly dies."

Ron asked, "When will that be?"

"I can't say for sure. Probably less than twenty-four hours, maybe only two or three. She could keep breathing for a couple of days, but I doubt it."

Ron seemed to gather some last strength, enough to even smile at the girls. "That sounds good to me. How about you? Shall we take her home and let her die in her bed like she wanted?"

And that's what happened. Melissa was home within an hour. The hospice nurse was there and kept her comfortable. I hope Mandy and Jennifer had enough peaceful time with their mom that they could think of her in the next few months without seeing messy blood and seizure contortions.

At the age of thirty-eight, Melissa Blackburn quietly died of metastatic lung cancer, surrounded by her family, about thirty-six hours after arriving home from the ER.

TERMINAL ILLNESS AND THE COMPASSION PROTOCOL

For many patients going through this slow, painful decline due to end-stage cancer, their worst fear is the effect their illness has on their family. Proud, private people may be terrified at the thought of someone, even a loved one, having to feed them, clean them, and even change their diapers. Providing twenty-four-hour care may be a sacrifice they are not willing to ask of their family. The last thing many people want is to end up living through a slow decline in a nursing home because their illness has overwhelmed their family's ability to care for them.

Consider the suffering of patients with end-stage cancer, like Melissa Blackburn. Growing inside their bodies is an invasive mass that is eating at their bones, pressing on their vital organs, and consuming all their nutrition. Cancer can obstruct hollow organs, such as the bowel, causing painful stretching behind the obstruction and ending the essential function of the organ. Cancer may eat at bone, causing intense pain as the bone is distorted and weakened, and eventually cause the collapse of the bone in pathological fractures. Cancer invades solid organs, replacing vital tissue with a nonfunctional tumor mass until the solid organ can't perform its function.

Understandably, many terminally ill patients reach a point where the pain and suffering of illness make life no longer worth living. The rapid metabolism of cancer can eat away at body tissue. First, fat is consumed and then muscle, until only skin and bones remain. During this catabolic state, a cancer patient has little extra energy for the enjoyment of life. Eventually, it is a chore just to stay awake and breathe.

CURRENT PRACTICES

Terminally ill patients are often more vulnerable to acute illnesses—that is, illnesses such as an infection or influenza that come on suddenly and can be treated in a short period of time. Such acute illnesses can cause these patients, whose bodies are already struggling to function, to become unresponsive or fall into a coma.

It is common for terminally ill patients to be in and out of the hospital for the treatment of acute illnesses. When patients become less responsive, their caretakers will almost always send them to the doctor for exhaustive (and sometimes painful) testing to diagnose the reason for their decreased mental status. Even if they have filled out an Advance Directive, they most likely will still be sent to their doctor's office or the ER.

Of those sent to the doctor, some patients will never recover from their acute illness despite medical intervention and will die in the hospital. But most will recover from their decreased mental status—the infection will be found, dehydration will be treated with intravenous fluids, or an electrolyte imbalance will be corrected. Patients are likely to be hospitalized for treatment until they can be sent home (or back to their nursing home) to continue their inevitable decline toward death.

For many terminally ill patients this vicious cycle repeats itself through hospitalization after hospitalization. In her emergency medicine practice, Dr. Fitzpatrick often encounters terminally ill cancer patients. They are brought in by a caring relative or sent in by ambulance with a note from their nursing home staff that they were found to have a fever, are just not themselves, or are coughing or short of breath.

The workup of these patients is fairly routine. They will have blood tests that check their electrolytes, their kidney and liver functions, their blood count, the therapeutic levels of any medications they are taking, and cultures of their blood. They will have a catheter passed into their bladder to collect urine to look for infection. They will have a chest X-ray. If all these tests are normal, they may have a CT scan of the brain to look for a stroke or bleed.

All this testing may take place even when patients have Advance Directives because the Advance Directive may be written in a way that it applies only if the patient is unresponsive. Often, some minor reversible illness is found—a urinary tract infection or pneumonia. Or the change in the patient's condition may be the result of fluid overload on a cardiovascular system that is worn out and barely carrying on, or it may be the result of a temporary drug toxicity.

Patients with such ailments will be admitted to the hospital to treat their acute conditions, and after two or three days they will return to their home or nursing home. Many of the patients Dr. Fitzpatrick sees have been stuck in this cycle for months or even years, with visits becoming gradually more frequent as the patients become more debilitated.

What will probably be missing from these patients' evaluations is a frank question about the goal of treatment. Do these patients still want curative treatment despite their advancing illness? Are they still glad to wake up in the morning? Do they know they have the option of quitting curative care and allowing a natural death?

The economic impact of a long, slow death can also make the difference between leaving adequate financial security for your loved ones and worrying about how your family will survive after you are gone. Phyllis Shattuck's husband, Robert, had to sell everything he owned, including their house, and it still took him years to pay the bill for Phyllis's six weeks in the hospital.

COMPASSION PROTOCOL PRACTICES

Our Compassion Protocol offers patients an opportunity to opt out of this cycle. First, we draw a distinction between being terminally ill, which is currently a narrowly defined legal term, and having a terminal illness. With the Compassion Protocol, if you have a terminal illness and your suffering has become intolerable, you may choose to let natural death occur sooner rather than later.

Patients whose quality of life has deteriorated to the point where they would prefer to die are aware that they will die soon in any event and that their good days are over. They have the right to put their affairs in order, say good-bye to their family and friends, give up the good fight, and allow death to occur naturally.

Unfortunately, few patients in this situation know that they have the option of Comfort Care Only—that they can opt out of curative care and take advantage of their next possible exit event. Most of their families and caregivers also lack that knowledge. It is amazing but overwhelmingly true that dying people do not talk with their families about dying—about how or when or where they want to die, or even about *if* they'll die—even at a point where it should be obvious. Dr. Fitzpatrick is often the first one to raise the issue with patients and their families. Her favorite way to do it with a patient who seems trapped in a life she might not want is just to say, "Louise, may I ask you a personal question? Are you glad to wake up every morning? Is there any part of you that hopes when you go to sleep at night that maybe you won't wake up?" Dr. Fitzpatrick has found that this question can be safely ignored by someone who is not ready—the person can easily pretend not to understand it—but it can also open a door to a discussion of end-of-life care with the patient and the patient's family.

Using the Compassion Protocol, patients with a terminal illness can ask their caretakers and the medical establishment to allow them to die without interference. Your options, should you decide to pursue the Compassion Protocol, are explained in chapter 6, Step One: Know Your Options. Patients continue to receive pain medication in doses that will keep them comfortable, as well as medication for anxiety if they need it. They will receive oxygen to ease the work of breathing. And they will be kept as comfortable as possible with good care for their fragile skin.

What they will *not* receive is another curative trip to the hospital. The next time they have a fever or just aren't themselves, they will be kept comfortable in their own beds. If they so choose, no tests will be done, no antibiotics will be given, and no intravenous hydration will be administered. No one will call 911 if they stop breathing or lose consciousness, and they will not be taken to the Emergency Room.

In addition, many of their routine daily medications may be discontinued. Heart medicine, insulin, and blood pressure medication help keep people going, often for years longer than they would have lived otherwise. Discontinuing such daily medications allows Compassion Protocol patients to die within a shorter period of time.

Persons with a terminal illness who choose the Compassion Protocol have decided that the end, when it comes, will be a merciful relief. If they so choose, these patients will be allowed to take advantage of their next exit event.

We have already looked at the sentient elderly and at persons with terminal illnesses, two groups who may benefit from using the Compassion Protocol. We turn now to those with Alzheimer's dementia who make plans for a natural death in the early stages of their disease.

CHAPTER FIVE

ALZHEIMER'S DEMENTIA AND THE COMPASSION PROTOCOL

Patients with Alzheimer's dementia are the third group for whom the Compassion Protocol is designed. At first glance this group may look the most troubling: If the Compassion Protocol works as it is intended, caregivers will be withholding curative care from patients who are wholly without the capacity to direct what is happening to them. Caregivers may also be asked to withhold care from people whose minds are gone but whose bodies are still far from death.

The obvious problem with Alzheimer's patients is that they are no longer mentally capable of making their own decisions. For this group, advance planning is critical. Should you wish to choose the Compassion Protocol if you become demented, preparing carefully before the onset of dementia is essential. If you do not have a Health Care Decision Maker, the options of the Compassion Protocol may not be available. If you have one appointed through other legal forms, then the Compassion Protocol will make it much easier for them to enforce your end-of-life decisions, including ceasing curative care.

In the following pages Dr. Fitzpatrick tells the story of Carl

Novack and how she and attorney Fitzpatrick came to believe that the Alzheimer's patient may be the most profound beneficiary of the Compassion Protocol.

DR. FITZPATRICK TELLS
CARL NOVACK'S STORY

Something special happens in a small Emergency Room gearing up for a code or serious trauma. Everything switches up a notch when the report comes in over the radio that an ambulance is coming in code four—with a cardiac arrest, serious motor vehicle accident, or respiratory arrest.

First, my blood pressure and pulse go up in response to the adrenaline that surges through my body. Then the level of activity in the ER goes up as the lab technician, respiratory therapist, X-ray technician, and two or three extra nurses arrive. Each person has his or her own designated task in a code, and for a few minutes they are all very busy checking their equipment, putting on protective masks and gowns, opening the crash cart, and seeking a state of perfect readiness.

Then, inevitably, there are a few more minutes of calm before the storm while we wait for the ambulance to arrive. There is excitement in the air; people are bouncing on their toes. I suspect it's a lot like being backstage before the curtain rises or warming up before a championship game.

Early in my career I was slightly offended by the excitement even though I couldn't help feeling it myself. It seemed slightly ghoulish, as if people were somehow enjoying someone else's tragedy. With experience I understood that the excitement comes from facing together the most extreme challenge to our skills and competence and knowing that we are about to be offered the chance to save a life by being good at what we do.

Once I'm sure we're as ready as we can be, I usually go outside to the ambulance bay to wait for the ambulance. It gives me a chance to take a few deep breaths by myself and focus.

It was in the ambulance bay that I first met Carl Novack. The ambulance screamed into the bay with flashing lights and sirens, and the back doors popped open. I stepped up on the bumper for a quick look as the crew prepared to bring the patient and all his attached equipment into the ER.

I already knew from the radio report that Carl was sixty-two years old, had choked on his lunch, and had a respiratory arrest. I knew from the pickup address that he was a resident at the local nursing home. The paramedics had related in their report that when they arrived Carl was apneic (not breathing), dark blue, and unresponsive, but his heart was still beating. The paramedics intubated Carl, bagged him with high-flow oxygen, started an IV, and transported him to the ER.

CARL'S CLEARLY EXPRESSED
RIGHT TO DIE IS VIOLATED

On first glance Carl looked about his stated age, slightly overweight (still well nourished), and now pink from the oxygen he had received from the ambulance. He was breathing on his own and was trying to move his arms, but they were tied to the gurney. The cardiac monitor lying at the foot of the gurney showed a sinus tachycardia (regular rapid heartbeat). Carl's puffy, pasty appearance is common in bedridden people whose muscles don't work hard enough to support their circulation. He had an endotracheal tube in his lungs, and one of the paramedics held the bag that delivered oxygen. I took the fat envelope holding Carl's nursing home chart from the paramedic and headed back inside.

When I opened the envelope, the first thing that fell out was Carl's Oregon POLST form. For those patients who have chosen to sign a Physician Orders for Life-Sustaining Treatment, the POLST form accompanies them whenever they are transported to any other facility.

The POLST form is bright pink so it can be easily found, and it is always hung at the foot of the patient's bed. The prominence of the form is designed to make it easier for first responders—the paramedics, in Carl's case—to follow its direction when the patient has an emergency.

Carl's form clearly stated that he wanted Comfort Care Only. I was already familiar with Comfort Care Only as defined by the Oregon POLST form:

> The patient/resident is treated with dignity, respect and kept clean, warm and dry. Reasonable measures are made to offer food and fluids by mouth, and attention is paid to hygiene. Medication, positioning, wound care and other measures are used to relieve pain and suffer-

ing. Oxygen, suction and manual treatment of airway obstruction may be used as needed for comfort. These measures are to be used where the patient/resident lives. The patient/resident is not to be hospitalized unless comfort measures fail.

I looked quickly through the rest of Carl's chart, learning that Alzheimer's dementia was his only diagnosis. He had been in the nursing home for eight years—the first six years in the assisted living section, and the last two years in the full care section.

Carl had a remarkably short medication list, taking only stool softeners, laxatives, and some psychiatric medications: Haldol, often given to ease aggression in the demented, a sedative at bedtime, and Valium as needed if he became agitated. His diagnosis read "end-stage Alzheimer's dementia."

Carl's right to die had just been seriously violated. If his nursing home had complied with his wishes, clearly stated on the POLST form, he would have already died. Instead, Carl was breathing on his own, had a strong heartbeat, had an invasive tube in his lungs and an intravenous line in his arm, and was restrained with his arms tied to the gurney so he couldn't interfere with his treatment.

He was moaning loudly and occasionally shouting, probably from pain, as oxygenated blood returned to tissue damaged during his apneic episode. The poor man, I thought.

While I was leafing through the chart, Carl was being transferred to an ER gurney. Everyone hovered around him, moving cardiac leads from the ambulance monitor to ours, checking IVs, and changing the oxygen hookup.

Without comment I took a 10-cc syringe, deflated the cuff on his endotracheal tube, and pulled it out of his mouth. He still breathed on his own, but he was now disconnected from the oxygen. All activity stopped, and everyone looked at me.

I said, "He has advanced Alzheimer's and a POLST form that clearly says he wants Comfort Care Only." I kept my voice calm as I asked the paramedics, "Why did you intubate him?"

Jim, the lead paramedic on the run, also worked as a tech in the ER and knew me well. He said, "He arrested in the dining room, and his POLST form wasn't there. He looks young and he wasn't breathing, so I intubated him. That's what I'm trained to do. Once the tube's in, I can't pull it out without a doctor's order."

Jim had acted correctly. The nursing home staff should never have called the paramedics. Carl had been there eight years with his bright pink POLST form sitting at the end of his bed and "Comfort Care Only" clearly marked on it. Let's assume the call was an honest mistake, perhaps by a new nurse who wasn't familiar with all the patients yet. Still, once the paramedics arrived, a nurse should have corrected the error by telling them that Carl was a DNR and should not be resuscitated.

The responsibility for violating Carl's right to die lay entirely on the nursing home. I was appalled but not surprised. Nursing home staff frequently disregard patients' wishes as explicitly stated by DNR, POLST, or Comfort Care Only orders. (See chapter 12, Everyone's Worst Fear: The Nursing Home, for a detailed discussion of this issue.)

The Difficult Medical
Care Decision—Again

While Jim and I were talking, all activity had stopped. The crew was still standing around Carl's bed, waiting. The lab technician was ready to draw blood and had a tourniquet on Carl's arm, needle poised over a vein, blood tubes in her hand. I released the tourniquet and told her we didn't need any labs right now, and she left. I told the X-ray technician to take the portable machine away and released her, too, along with the extra nurses.

The respiratory therapist had put a nasal cannula on Carl's nose to give him oxygen after I removed the tube. The therapist was trying to get a reading on the oxygen saturation monitor to see if Carl was getting enough oxygen. He adjusted the clip on Carl's finger and showed me the readout: 79 percent.

Carl's oxygen level was dangerously below the normal range of 92–98 percent, but I knew the reading was falsely low because of the hypoxic damage to Carl's tissue and vasoconstriction in his extremities. The respiratory therapist asked if he could put a PEEP mask on Carl's face. This is a plastic mask that sits an inch from the patient's face and has a tight seal around it, holding oxygen at high pressure to help the patient overcome airway resistance when he breathes.

I said, "I don't think so. Let's just leave him alone for now."

The therapist said, "It's not considered invasive and is accepted treatment in a DNR." I knew he was right. In fact, the PEEP mask had been developed to offer comfort care to patients in the ICU who have DNR requests.

Carl wasn't just a DNR, however; he had requested Comfort

Care Only. I did not think the PEEP mask would increase his comfort. In fact, I took the oxygen tube off his nose.

I asked the nurse to get some Valium and some morphine. Carl was still moaning loudly, shouting, and writhing on the bed. His eyes remained closed, and he showed no response to his environment. I could at least make him more comfortable with some medications.

I turned back to Jim and asked him if he knew whether any family had been notified. He didn't. I asked the ward clerk to call the nursing home and find out if they had contacted Carl's family. His chart told me he had a wife living in town, a daughter who lived nearby, and a son who lived about a hundred miles away.

The nurse returned with the medication. I ordered 5 milligrams of Valium and 10 milligrams of morphine IV, an amount that would sedate Carl and ease his pain. The nurse drew up the meds and put both doses into Carl's IV. Carl became calmer and was no longer moaning and crying out. He continued to take deep snoring breaths. His oxygen saturation still showed very low numbers. I put his nasal oxygen back on him.

When a POLST Form Fails

Carl's wife and daughter arrived, and I went to the hospital chapel to talk to them. The two very attractive, well-dressed women of indeterminate age looked like sisters. After introductions and my expression of sympathy, they asked me how he was.

"He's breathing on his own, and his heart is beating strongly.

He's not awake yet, and he's in a lot of pain, so I've given him some medication to make him comfortable."

They asked me what had happened. I told them that Carl had had a respiratory arrest, the nursing home called 911, and the paramedics intubated him and cleared his airway so he could breathe again. Carl's wife, Laurel, began sobbing and moaning, "No, no! Poor Carl. No, no more."

Carl's daughter, Lynn, asked me, "Do you mean he was dying, but they didn't let him die?" I told her yes, that was what had happened.

She spoke through barely controlled anger and pain: "How could this happen? Dad had a POLST form requesting Comfort Care Only. Why were the paramedics even called?"

I had no good answer for her questions. Nursing homes' disregard of Comfort Care Only forms is an ongoing problem—this was not the first time I had faced angry family members when a POLST form was ignored. The only thing I could offer Lynn was that her father's POLST form wasn't with him when he went into arrest, that the paramedics did the right thing when they arrived, and that the mix-up happened because his POLST form was back by his bed—a not uncommon problem.

Later that day, after I felt that my anger was under control, I called the nursing home to ask them about Carl. I wanted to try to understand what had happened. I talked to the charge nurse who had been on duty earlier when Carl arrested.

After identifying myself, I asked her, "Carl's POLST form clearly calls for Comfort Care Only, so why was 911 called and why was he resuscitated?"

She was silent for several seconds, clearly thinking about my question. It turned out that she was not trying to explain a mistake—she was genuinely perplexed as to why I was asking such a thing.

After some consideration, her response was "But we have no terminal diagnosis on Mr. Novack." She considered that statement an adequate explanation of what had transpired. To her mind Carl's request for Comfort Care Only didn't apply unless he had a terminal diagnosis. Even though he had been living a life he clearly didn't want to live for at least two years, it was the nursing home's policy to keep him alive as long as possible.

I LEARN ABOUT THE MAN CARL WAS

Over the next two hours I learned that Carl Novack had been a professor of political science at the local university. Lynn told me that he was a very happy man, much loved by his students.

When his memory began to fade at such a young and still active age, Carl's main concern was what his progressing Alzheimer's would do to his wife. He made the arrangements to move into a nursing home by himself while he was still competent. He wanted his wife to get on with her life, not to spend her prime years caring for him. Mostly, Lynn said, Carl hoped for an early death.

"My father was a humble man," she said, "but his intelligence was very important to him. He would not at all like to be alive as he is now. I know if he had any consciousness left, he would be imploring us to just let him die."

Instead, Carl had spent the last four years becoming progressively demented. He had not recognized his family for two years. He couldn't talk now and didn't move at all unless prompted. He could still feed himself if someone sat by him and helped him. He couldn't dress or bathe himself. He wore a diaper. He remained mostly docile, rarely suffering the aggressive or violent outbursts of many Alzheimer's patients.

CARL'S MISSED EXIT EVENT

When I took them in to see Carl, the first thing Lynn said was "What's the oxygen for?"

I told her he still wasn't moving air very well, and it was helping him get enough oxygen.

She asked, "Is it keeping him alive?"

I didn't know the answer to that. Yes, without it he might deoxygenate enough to put his heart into a dysrhythmia. But without the oxygen now he could suffer more brain damage if he survived the day. Lynn and her mother asked me to take it off.

Carl and his family spent two more hours in the Emergency Room. I sat with Laurel when I could, just listening to her talk about Carl in his good days. Lynn was in and out and on the phone. Her brother arrived. He had more questions and more anger about what might have been and why it didn't work.

Carl recovered from his missed exit event. He stayed in the hospital for two days, treated only for comfort. His primary care doctor had known Carl a long time and was nearly as angry as the family at what had happened. He admitted Carl with nasal oxygen supplementation, however, and he checked lab tests each day and gave him IV fluid support.

The family considered terminating his residency at the nursing home and taking Carl home. They had the resources to provide the twenty-four-hour nursing care he would need if he went home. They knew that at home they could let him stop eating and let him die sooner. But they ended up deciding to honor Carl's wishes that he not be cared for like a child by the wife whom he wanted to remember him as the man he was.

After two days Carl was back to his baseline, and he returned to the nursing home. He lived another eighteen months and then died in the hospital of pneumonia and cardiac arrest.

ALZHEIMER'S DEMENTIA AND THE COMPASSION PROTOCOL

Alzheimer's is a slowly progressive neurological deterioration that affects the so-called higher functions of the brain. Chief among these are reason, memory, and intellect. The classic picture of advanced Alzheimer's is a person with the mind of a two-year-old and a fairly healthy body who is increasingly unable to remember anything and eventually becomes unable to communicate or to be left unsupervised for even a few minutes. The vital centers of the brain—those controlling the heart, lungs, kidneys, and blood flow—are affected only very late in the progression of the disease.

Because the disease begins and progresses so slowly, most Alzheimer's patients encounter the medical community while they are still competent enough to make their own decisions. If they have not already done so, this is the point at which patients should consider and confirm what they want the final years of their lives to be like.

Subsequent chapters will take you through the five steps of the Compassion Protocol, whereby you can consider your choices and increase control over what you want your end-of-life medical care to be.

Many people are committed to fighting death to the last breath, no matter the circumstances—sentient or not, despite any imaginable level of incapacity, pain, or suffering. We have talked with people who feel that we are given only one span of life on this planet and that we should not deprive ourselves of a single possible breath. We say, more power to them.

If you decide, however, that you would not want to spend years in the prolonged decline of Alzheimer's dementia, you can sign the Compassion Protocol while you are still mentally sound and ask to be allowed the natural death that comes to the infirm. The time to do so is before mental incapacity renders you unable to choose.

As we shall see, patients in the early stage of Alzheimer's who choose the Compassion Protocol appoint a Health Care Decision Maker and sign a Contract for Compassionate Care (appendix A). The Health Care Decision Maker's job is to ensure that the patient's wishes are carried out once the patient slips into dementia.

We must emphasize here that the choice of Comfort Care Only will be available to the Alzheimer's patient only under two possible circumstances. The first circumstance occurs when the patient has signed a Contract for Compassionate Care or other

Advanced Directive with his or her medical providers, which includes the appointment of a Health Care Decision Maker. The contract explicitly indicates the patient's choice for the discontinuation of curative care under narrowly controlled circumstances, discussed in detail in chapter 9, Step Four: Do the Paperwork.

The second circumstance whereby the cessation of curative care will be available is when the patient has not done the paperwork but his family and friends can present clear and convincing evidence that the patient would choose the Comfort Care Only if he were able. If you are mentally incapacitated, no one can choose withdrawal from curative care for you. Either you have already chosen for yourself or you have indicated, clearly and convincingly, that this is your choice. With Alzheimer's dementia on the rise, the Compassion Protocol is an option that people should begin to consider in early middle age.

The Compassion Protocol offers people with early Alzheimer's dementia increased assurance that their wishes will be carried out. Many people, including Carl Novack, know that they want to die when their reason and intellect are gone, rather than wait until the disease affects their heart or lungs. They have the option of choosing to allow an exit event to cause a natural death at an early point in their mental deterioration instead of waiting years for their illness to overwhelm modern medicine's ability to keep them alive.

At the point that your agreement takes effect, it will be your choices and not your caretaker's that determine your treatment. The agreement will specify your wishes—for example, that curative care ceases and Comfort Care Only begins when you are no longer able to feed yourself. Or you might choose to have comfort care begin when you reach a point that you require assistance twenty-four hours a day and can't be left alone, or when a year has passed since you last recognized your loved ones. The agreement may specify that your Health Care Decision Maker can decide to institute Comfort Care Only at any time after you are no longer able to choose for yourself.

You will have chosen while you were still competent to make your own decisions precisely what treatment you will or will not receive. Your Health Care Decision Maker will then put your choices into effect under carefully crafted, specific circumstances.

IS THIS REALLY LEGAL?

The two principles necessary to extend Comfort Care Only to those with Alzheimer's dementia who have prepared for a natural death are already well established. First, we have the right to determine the course of our own medical care when we are mentally capable. Second, we have the right and ability to plan for our wishes to be carried out through Advance Directives and a Power of Attorney for Health Care. The validity of these documents has already been tested and upheld, and some states already allow for such things as the withholding of nutrition.

It is worthwhile at this point to state clearly that the Compassion Protocol is never available to persons with mental retardation. By definition, the mentally retarded lack legal capacity; for example, they cannot enter into contracts. In allowing Alzheimer's patients to choose the Compassion Protocol while still mentally competent, we draw a sharp distinction between Alzheimer's patients and people with mental retardation. The Compassion Protocol is in essence a contract—a social contract with you, your loved ones, and your health care providers. Because of the potential for abuse and because there is no legal way to be certain of the wishes of persons with mental retardation, this vulnerable group must always be presumed to choose life at any cost.

In contrast, the early Alzheimer's patient does possess legal capacity and may enter into the Compassion Protocol while still mentally competent. It is important to complete the Compassion Protocol paperwork as early as possible to ensure your right to determine your end-of-life care.

The legal basis of the Compassion Protocol is liable to face spirited opposition from those who believe that life should always be preserved under any circumstances. But we feel strongly that allowing the extreme elderly, persons with a terminal illness, and end-stage Alzheimer's patients to die of natural causes sooner rather than later constitutes a return to the rhythms of life and death that governed human existence through the millennia until the discovery of penicillin. Rather than taking us into new and uncharted legal territory, what we really embrace are the processes that have "shuffled us off this mortal coil" for thousands of years.

UPDATING TIME-HONORED ADVICE

Our aunt Iona was a head nurse in hospitals during World War II and for thirty years after. She gave us some memorable advice in our youth, wisdom based on her inside knowledge of doctors and hospitals.

Aunt Iona said, "If you ever get really sick, visit the doctor to find out what it is. Then go home and lock the door!" She had seen too many miserable, lonely, sterile hospital deaths unnecessarily prolonged by what she considered an uncaring medical system.

Aunt Iona's advice reminds us that we always have the option of staying home and not seeking medical care. Unfortunately, the stay-at-home approach also deprives us of much-needed medical comfort at the end of life.

We have come a long way since Aunt Iona's nursing career, especially with the growth of the hospice movement. But as you have seen, the problems that Auntie warned us about are still with us today. The Carl Novacks of this world still routinely receive CPR against their wishes, and the Melissa Blackburns are far more likely to breathe their last breath surrounded by beeping medical machinery than at home with their families and loved ones. Nearly every person we have talked with in our years of wrestling with this problem has a story of a family member or friend whose suffering was unnecessarily protracted at the end of life.

We developed the Compassion Protocol to address and solve this problem of how to let death take place sooner rather than later, at home or in a venue of your choice, with all possible medical care administered to provide comfort. We hope Aunt Iona would agree that the Compassion Protocol is a good answer to her disillusionment with the medical system's handling of death.

The following chapters explain in detail how the five steps of the Compassion Protocol work. Specific instructions are given for each of the three groups that can benefit from the Compassion Protocol: the competent elderly, the terminally ill, and those with Alzheimer's dementia who have previously chosen a natural death.

HOW THE COMPASSION PROTOCOL WORKS

Until the mid-twentieth century, elderly people eventually got sick, took to their beds, and died. As a result of modern medicine, people are living longer and staying healthy and active to a more advanced age. We all still die, but now we die about fifteen years later than people did a century ago. Along with our improved health and longevity has come the institutionalization of our elderly: Many of them live in nursing homes and die in hospitals, often months or years after they have stopped enjoying life.

You will probably fight against death for as long as you can, and your doctors will do everything possible to keep you alive and healthy. Like many people, however, you may eventually reach the point where your doctor can keep you alive, but you have lost your ability to live independently or are living in unbearable pain or are descending into dementia.

If you get to that point, you no longer have to let your doctors and loving family members continue to interfere with your chance for a natural death. Over the years many patients have said to Dr. Fitzpatrick, "Please let me die," but no one has ever asked her, "How can I die?" There are many excellent books on the problem of death in our society, books that call for change and a more compassionate approach to death, but none of them provides simple, actual steps that can be taken to gain access to a natural death.

We have written this book to present the Compassion Protocol, a tool you can use when you no longer want to fight for life. If you outlive your enjoyment of life, you can decide that you are ready to take advantage of your next possible exit event and use the Compassion Protocol to make sure a natural death is allowed to occur.

The Five Steps of the Compassion Protocol

1. Know your options.
2. Make your decisions.
3. Communicate your decisions.
4. Do the paperwork.
5. Prepare for a natural death.

As you go through the steps of the Compassion Protocol, you will be making critical life decisions. The second half of this book focuses on educating you about the choices you will make and the consequences of those choices. When you complete the Contract for Compassionate Care (appendix A), you must be fully informed of what you are doing and capable of making rational decisions. The more you document that you have carefully considered all your end-of-life alternatives and have chosen the Compassion Protocol after being fully informed of the consequences of your decision, the more successfully your choices will be implemented when the time is right.

When you reach the point that you are ready to allow a natural death to occur, you may not be able, mentally or physically, to go through the five steps of the Compassion Protocol. Chances are, especially in the era of Alzheimer's dementia, that your Health Care Decision Maker will be the one who tells the doctors what your wishes are and when it is time to cease curative care. That person will be the one who enforces your choices with your doctors, family members, or nursing home personnel. But that person cannot initiate the Compassion Protocol unless you have made the decisions for yourself at a time when you were still mentally competent.

To see how each of the steps in the Compassion Protocol works, we will revisit the end-of-life stories that Dr. Fitzpatrick has told of her patients and see how those stories can turn out differently when the patient employs the steps available through the Compassion Protocol.

CHAPTER SIX

STEP ONE:
KNOW YOUR OPTIONS

As we have discussed, the Compassion Protocol is based on the withdrawal of curative care and the application of all available comfort care. In Step One of the Compassion Protocol you learn what your choices are for withdrawal of care at the end of life, choices that you may not have considered before. Curative care can be withheld through the following options when you or your Health Care Decision Maker decide you are ready for a natural death.

Your End-of-Life Options

1. Don't go to the hospital again.

2. Refuse antibiotics.

3. Discontinue your usual medications.

4. Refuse hydration and nutrition.

Let's return to Willa Simpson to see what she might have considered when it came to her end-of-life options if the Compassion Protocol had been available to her.

Willa Simpson, as you will recall, was a ninety-two-year-old woman from the local nursing home. She falls into the first of our three categories: the sentient elderly. All Willa wanted to do, according to her stated wishes, was drift off to sleep and not wake up. The nursing home had been forcing her to eat, to the point of actually prying her jaw open to make her take food or liquids. In her twenty years of practice Dr. Fitzpatrick has often encountered patients like Willa: the extreme elderly, often with little family left, who have long been bedridden, who have long been confined to a nursing home, and who no longer want to continue living.

If Willa had elected to follow the Compassion Protocol, Step One would have been for her to Know Her Options. Our Contract for Compassionate Care (see appendix A or visit www.compassionprotocol.org) is a legally binding contract signed by you, your Health Care Decision Maker, and your primary care physician. Part II, entitled Options, contains the same list as shown above. When Willa began to consider her end-of-life care, her first step would have been to work through this list of decision points and come to understand them.

OPTION ONE: DON'T GO TO THE HOSPITAL AGAIN

At the time Dr. Fitzpatrick saw her, Willa did not want to be in the ER. Her nursing home had sent her to the ER because she was exhibiting an altered mental state: She had stopped eating and drinking on her own, was sleeping large parts of the day, and had become less cooperative and responsive. Unless you choose option one—to not go to the hospital again—you will be transported to the hospital under these circumstances, as Willa was.

Other reasons to be taken to the hospital include developing a fever, becoming confused (altered mental state again), becoming short of breath, or developing pneumonia or a urinary tract infection. These are the most common reasons that your nursing home or caregiver might call for paramedic transport to the hospital or ER. Each one of these conditions can be a potential exit event; if left untreated, the condition could lead to your death in a matter of days.

If you choose not to go to the hospital again to receive curative care, you will be treated in your own bed, at the nursing home, at a hospice, or at home (where you should seek the care of a hospice nurse; see chapter 11). Treatment will be given as needed to keep you comfortable, but nothing will be done to interfere with a possible exit event.

However, even if all your paperwork is in order and your family understands that you don't want curative treatment, you are still likely to receive it if you go to the hospital. In the Emergency Room those in extremis will be treated first and asked about their wishes later. Remember that in most busy Emergency Rooms, Willa Simpson would have had a battery of tests before seeing the doctor. Doctors have a very hard time letting people die. Even when it doesn't seriously conflict with their religious beliefs, letting people die runs counter to all their training. It is also possible that some doctors may think they are legally required to treat any curable condition, but they are not.

Simple treatments such as oxygen, intravenous hydration, or antibiotics can prevent a possible exit event from bringing you the natural death you have decided you want. If you go to the ER, you may miss your chance for an exit event and prolong your suffering unnecessarily.

The best way to avoid unwanted life-prolonging treatment is to stay out of the Emergency Room. But even if you end up in the ER, there are other options to help you achieve a natural death.

OPTION TWO: REFUSE ANTIBIOTICS

Another option for Willa that goes hand-in-hand with the decision not to go to the ER is the decision to refuse antibiotics that are used to treat infections. The two most common that bedridden patients contract are pneumonia and urinary tract infections, both of which occur as a direct consequence of physical changes that take place in the body as a result of long-term reduced mobility.

We mentioned earlier how pneumonia used to be called "the old man's friend" because it was a common and relatively easy exit event for the extreme elderly. Pneumonia occurs easily among people at the end of life because weak muscles make successful coughing difficult, so normal fluids pool in the lungs and are colonized by bacteria.

Similarly, anyone wearing a diaper for incontinence is subject to frequent urinary tract infections. Particularly in women, the moisture of a diaper increases the number of bacteria on the skin, and if those bacteria get into the bladder, they cause an infection. An untreated bladder infection rapidly becomes a kidney infection as the bacteria migrate from the bladder to the kidneys.

Either of these infections, if left untreated, is likely to spread to the bloodstream. In healthy people the body's immune system can usually defeat such an infection and return the person to good health. Because the extreme elderly, the terminally ill, and the bedridden Alzheimer's patient (each of our Compassion Protocol groups) have depressed immune systems, the infection can become life-threatening if left untreated.

Death by infection can be considered a relatively peaceful, quiet death. As the fever climbs, the patient becomes confused or sleepy and spends less time awake. If the patient can answer questions, more often than not that patient will say he or she is feeling all right and has no pain.

As the infection continues untreated, the patient will slip deeper into a coma over the next few days. Soon the blood supply to the brain will fall below that required to sustain the heart and lungs. The patient will die of cardiovascular collapse—a drop in blood pressure caused by the infection.

The death from an untreated infection is the classic picture of the "good death" so popular in nineteenth-century and Victorian novels, such as Beth's death in *Little Women* or in any novel by Dickens. Beth's death was untimely and tragic, but it took place at home with her family gathered around her deathbed. They comforted her as she reaffirmed her family's spiritual values of hope beyond death. In *Little Women* such a death is terribly sad. For one who is suffering horribly, it can also bring a merciful release.

In some states the option to refuse antibiotics is now part of Advance Directive forms—but your choice will most likely be implemented only if you have been diagnosed as terminally ill by two doctors. As we have discussed, doctors are justifiably reluctant to designate someone as terminally ill because the diagnosis itself may hasten death if it ends a patient's hope for improvement.

End-stage cancer patients easily receive the necessary "terminally ill" diagnosis from their doctor. But many others approaching death from heart failure, stroke, Alzheimer's dementia, or simple failure to thrive are unlikely to be defined as terminally ill.

Willa Simpson was neither terminally ill nor in a coma, and withholding antibiotics was not an option for her at that time. One of the main benefits of the Compassion Protocol is that it addresses this issue head-on. Our Contract for Compassionate Care (appendix A) specifically states that the various options you consider in Step One for end-of-life care do not require a diagnosis of terminal illness in order to be implemented. That is, your right to refuse medical care is not dependent on your diagnosis. The Compassion Protocol extends the legal right to refuse medical treatment to end-of-life patients if that is their choice, whether they have been diagnosed as terminally ill or not.

If you reach the point in your illness where life gives more suffering than it is humanly possible to endure, you can make that simple request: Give me no more antibiotics under any circumstances except upon a specific request from me.

OPTION THREE: DISCONTINUE
YOUR USUAL MEDICATIONS

The third option Willa may consider is to discontinue her usual medications. Willa was on a whole list of regular meds, as are many of the extreme elderly, taking ten to fifteen different prescriptions daily. Some are for the heart, keeping it in a regular, strong rhythm. Some are for blood pressure. Willa was on cholesterol-lowering medications designed to prevent the development of atherosclerosis and to protect her against the heart disease that may or may not develop as a result of her high cholesterol. Many other extreme elderly are on diabetes medications, both oral forms and insulin.

All these medications were important in keeping Willa healthy for the past twenty years or more. They delayed the natural aging process, which is a good thing—except when it isn't. If you decide that delaying death causes more suffering than allowing a natural death to occur sooner rather than later, you may choose to discontinue those medications that work only to delay the natural aging process rather than contribute to your comfort.

As you will remember, Drs. Fitzpatrick and Street wrote orders discontinuing Willa Simpson's daily maintenance medications. Willa was ready to die—indeed, it was her stated preference to be left alone so she could do just that—and under those circumstances she didn't want to take those meds that were designed to help her keep living longer.

Unless you are diabetic, stopping your medications may have little immediate effect. Discontinuing heart and blood pressure medications is unlikely to cause you discomfort. You might not notice any effects. But continuing those medications may be preventing heart dysrhythmias, which can bring a potential exit event in the form of sudden cardiac arrest. Many heart medications can prevent sudden cardiac death. Stopping the medications will not cause a cardiac arrest, but it will allow one to happen if your heart is sufficiently tired and weak.

Stopping insulin or oral hypoglycemic medications will cause a rise in your blood sugar and, if your diabetes is severe, will eventually lead to coma and death. You will not be aware of your rising blood sugar but will gradually become more tired and weak until your diabetic coma allows you an exit event.

You may decide to stop many or all of these medications when you decide you are ready to die. Any medications that you take for comfort, such as pain relievers, muscle relaxers, stool softeners, sedatives, or antidepressants, can be continued.

This is a serious subject, and talking about steps you can take to allow coma and death to occur naturally makes many people uncomfortable. We are not used to talking about death in our society. It is as though we are all at a cocktail party chatting while we pointedly avoid mentioning the two-ton elephant in the middle of the room. Death will come to each of us, but we spend more time talking about and planning for a root canal than we do for the final, inevitable, and potentially most unpleasant event of our lives.

One of the purposes of the Compassion Protocol is to open a dialog about this very important topic. How do you want to die? What do you want your final days to be like? Wouldn't you like to influence how events unfold to the greatest extent possible?

When you no longer want to medicate your body to avoid death, you have the right to ask your caretakers to discontinue your usual medications except those designed to increase your comfort. This was a choice that Willa Simpson made with Drs. Fitzpatrick and Street. As it turned out in Willa's case, stopping her meds had little impact on the course of her final days. It was the following option that Willa was seeking.

OPTION FOUR: REFUSE HYDRATION AND NUTRITION

Willa Simpson had been trying to refuse hydration and nutrition on her own in the weeks prior to her presentation to Dr. Fitzpatrick in the ER. She was not voluntarily eating or drinking, and all she wanted to do was sleep. Nursing home personnel were trying to help her continue with fluids and food, to the point of prying her jaw open and making her swallow. It is a common myth that hunger and thirst are discomforts associated with dying that a loving family member or a caring nurse can easily prevent, often by aggressively offering food and fluids to someone who no longer wants them.

Those who stop eating and drinking altogether will die a reasonably comfortable death within a fairly short period of time. Like Willa, they will gradually slip into a coma and die within one or two weeks. This is a powerful choice if you are ready to die.

Death from lack of nutrition or fluids does not appear to be painful or unpleasant. In fact, the inability to eat is a natural part of progressive disease. The stomach and intestines gradually lose their ability to handle nutrition. Forcing food on someone at this point can cause abdominal discomfort, nausea, and pain.

Willa had actually lost her appetite. The thought and experience of food no longer appealed to her. Hunger is naturally lost as part of the dying process. A decision to stop eating is unlikely to cause much if any discomfort.

The same is true of thirst. Hospice patients are routinely asked if they are thirsty as part of the comfort care measures of palliative care. Those approaching death often say no, and those who say yes often get relief just by wetting their mouths.

What will happen if you stop eating and drinking? Much like Willa Simpson, you will gradually lose strength over a few days. You will spend more and more time sleeping, slip into a coma, and die.

For those who are at the end of a long illness, this choice may mean removal of a feeding tube or intravenous line. If you are in a nursing home, you may run into resistance, much like Willa Simpson did. It is critically important, therefore, when choosing a nursing home for yourself that you discuss with nursing home personnel the end-of-life options that are important to you. If you are choosing a nursing home for a loved one, ask about the end-of-life options that are important to that loved one and talk to the personnel at the nursing home. Make sure the nursing home you choose will respect your or your loved one's end-of-life wishes.

Some nursing homes consider nutrition to be basic care that

cannot be refused, but they are wrong. You or your Health Care Decision Maker have the legal right, when you are ready, to refuse hydration and nutrition.

HEALTH CARE OPTIONS SUMMARY

In Step One: Know Your Options we looked at these four options:

1. Don't go to the hospital again.
2. Refuse antibiotics.
3. Discontinue your usual medications.
4. Refuse hydration and nutrition.

As long as you are mentally competent, you have the legal right to choose how you will be cared for as you approach death. You can make your choices well in advance, while you're still healthy. If you do so as Step One of the Compassion Protocol, you will increase the likelihood that your wishes will be followed when the appropriate time comes.

If you are using the Compassion Protocol to plan for an unknown future at a time when you are still healthy, you need to be able to designate when you want your chosen options to go into effect. Willa obviously chose all the options immediately; she had been ready for death for some time. Most of us will designate a time in the future or a set of circumstances when we want to cease curative care and allow a natural death to occur. Only you can choose when the options of Step One will be adopted as part of your medical care. The following section discusses when that appropriate time might be.

CHOOSING WHEN YOUR OPTIONS TAKE EFFECT

Having read about the options available to her in these pages, Willa would not have completed her work on Step One until she understood her choices as to when the options would take effect. Anyone who makes these choices may specify that the options of Step One will take effect under one or more of the following six circumstances:

1. Immediately

This option can be chosen by those who feel they are ready now for a natural death. Your choices from Step One would begin immediately. Willa Simpson and Melissa Blackburn would have chosen this option. Carl Novack would have completed his paperwork before he was ready for death and therefore would not have made this choice.

2. Close to Death

This is a subjective standard. The Contract for Compassionate Care specifically states that only you or your Health Care Decision Maker can determine when you feel you are close to death.

For Willa Simpson this would have been an easy choice. Her contract would have specified that she chose each of the options discussed above and that the options would go into effect when she was close to death. The decision as to whether she was approaching death was made easy for Willa because her body was telling her that her span of years was coming to a close. Her appetite was gone. She didn't feel particularly thirsty. She wanted to sleep and resented the nurses waking her up all the time.

Under current medical practices if Willa had caught pneumonia, she probably would have been sent to the ER and started on antibiotics. She would still be receiving heart medication that might be preventing cardiac arrest. And the nursing home would most likely continue to feed and hydrate her.

By choosing to implement her options when she felt she was close to death, Willa would have been able to avoid unwanted trips to the ER. She would not have received curative care, food, or hydration. A natural death would have been allowed to occur sooner rather than later, without intervention to stave off what was inevitable at this point. Willa's need to exercise the options laid out in the Compassion Protocol ends here, but three other timing options offer hope to some of the other stories shared above.

3. Permanently Unconscious

This timing option is designed to prevent heroic measures (breathing tubes and machines) in the event you fall into a coma. The Advance Directives currently available generally provide for this choice but have been interpreted to require a terminal illness diagnosis. The Contract for Compassionate Care clarifies your decisions. For example, if you are in a coma but breathing on your own, your feeding tube will be removed if that is the choice you made.

History would have unfolded very differently with respect to the high-profile Right to Die cases if the choices in the Contract for Compassionate Care had been available to the victims. Terri Schiavo, the Florida woman whose coma served as a battleground for political grandstanding on both the Left and the Right, would have had her feeding tube quietly removed. Her name would not now be recognizable as that poor woman subjected to a huge court battle and untold publicity at the time of her death.

If Terri's family had sought action in the courts to prevent her wishes from being carried out, her Contract for Compassionate Care could have been introduced as "clear and convincing evidence" of her wishes, thus meeting the standards set forth by the U.S. Supreme Court in the Nancy Cruzan case.

The fourth timing option for when your end-of-life medical care choices take effect is this:

4. Advanced Progressive Illness

Melissa Blackburn is the obvious example of when this option might be critical. She was in the last stages of metastatic lung cancer. She was being cared for at home, and it was her and her family's wish that she be allowed to die at home. Given the advanced state of her disease, she would have had little difficulty finding two doctors willing to diagnose her as terminally ill.

Melissa's POLST form was sufficient to manage her care after she arrived at the ER, but if she had completed the Compassion Protocol, the last days of her life might not have resulted in a trip to the ER.

As you will recall, her sister had stepped out to do some shopping, leaving Melissa in the care of her two teenage daughters. Melissa suffered a grand mal seizure, and with blood pouring from Melissa's nose and mouth, the daughters called for an ambulance.

At this point it is important to remember that if your loved ones call for an ambulance, you will almost certainly be revived or resuscitated and rushed to the ER, no matter what choices and paperwork you have in place to the contrary.

The point at which the Compassion Protocol could have impacted Melissa's end-of-life experience was prior to this crisis. She and her family also would have completed Step Five, in which they planned for the death they wanted and specified the death they didn't want. Seizure is not uncommon in the last stages of advanced progressive illness, and Step Five would have helped Melissa's family prepare for that and other unpleasant events that could occur, preventing the panic that led her daughters to call the ambulance.

Additionally, if Melissa had gone through all five steps of the Compassion Protocol, she might have been able to take advantage of an earlier, less traumatic exit event. Being bedridden for some time, Melissa might have developed a urinary tract infection. If she had chosen to refuse antibiotic treatment, such an infection might have proven fatal. She and her family may have preferred an exit such as this to the protracted suffering she experienced instead.

Notice that this timing option does not require a diagnosis of terminal illness. A determination that you are suffering from an advanced progressive illness makes the options you choose (whether to refuse antibiotics, discontinue your usual medications, etc.) available to you at an earlier point in the progression of your disease.

But what of those illnesses that are debilitating and cause continuing escalating pain and suffering but progress along a more uncertain timeline?

5. Extraordinary Suffering

On November 14, 2004, millions of Americans watched *60 Minutes* on television while a doctor administered lethal injections to a man who was suffering from amyotrophic lateral sclerosis (ALS), commonly referred to as Lou Gehrig's disease. To put it bluntly, *60 Minutes* televised a doctor killing his patient.

Prior to showing the death itself, Mike Wallace let the patient appeal to the camera and to the home audience. The patient was not pleading for his life; he was explaining why he had chosen to die at the hands of his doctor, whom he made a point of thanking. He described how his lungs would fill up with fluid and his decreased muscular function made it increasingly difficult to clear his lungs by coughing. He told how he was in constant fear of choking to death and was afraid of the agony he would experience during those few terrifying minutes of slow suffocation before consciousness left.

Needless to say, this segment of the show was disturbing and, in the eyes of many, inexcusably grisly. We recount it here for two reasons.

First, this patient's daily life is an example of the extraordinary suffering one might experience in which it would be appropriate for Step One options to go into effect if that is desired. Other diseases that inflict extraordinary suffering but that might not merit a diagnosis of terminal or advanced progressive illness are advanced rheumatoid or degenerative arthritis, endstage liver disease, congestive heart failure, and obstructive pulmonary disease. In such cases patients might appropriately choose that their Step One options go into effect because of the extraordinary suffering they are experiencing.

Second, we believe that with the adoption of the Compassion Protocol, such patients are given more choice and control over their medical care in end-of-life situations. Death may be allowed to occur sooner rather than later, perhaps by untreated infection or by a cardiac event occurring when heart medications are discontinued. With increased choice and control, and by allowing natural death to occur in a possibly more timely manner, we believe patients will have less occasion to consider the drastic options of suicide or doctor-assisted suicide.

One timing option remains and perhaps describes the circumstances in which the Compassion Protocol will have the most profound effect.

6. Alzheimer's Dementia

If you have been diagnosed with Alzheimer's dementia, your Step One options will go into effect under circumstances you have discussed with your Health Care Decision Maker. Examples of such circumstances are being bedridden, being unable to care for yourself or feed yourself, or not being able to recognize family and friends for a period of one or more years.

For many people the specter of Alzheimer's dementia is the most feared end-of-life experience. While the patient himself often has little discomfort, especially in the early years, it can be overwhelming to contemplate the emotional pain and suffering the disease inflicts on loved ones. For many of us, hanging on to life at any cost while in the debilitating later years of Alzheimer's simply makes no sense.

We will now reconsider the story of Carl Novack as an example of how the Compassion Protocol can work in the life of an Alzheimer's patient.

Carl Novack, a university professor with a vibrant and active social and family life, first began to experience short-term memory problems while still in his late forties. Over the course of the next two years the diagnosis was confirmed that he was experiencing the early stages of Alzheimer's dementia.

After countless hours of discussion with his family and consultations with his doctors, Carl reached a decision. He did not want the progression of his illness to devastate his family, and he did not want his beloved wife's memories of him to be clouded by years of having to care for him as though he were an infant. At this point, following the Compassion Protocol, Carl would decide which of the Step One options he would like employed in his end-of-life care. For Carl the choice would be easy. He would choose all four options:

1. Don't go to the hospital again.
2. Refuse antibiotics.
3. Discontinue your usual medications.
4. Refuse hydration and nutrition.

As to when these options should be employed, notice that the timing options we have already considered might not serve Carl's purpose:

1. Immediately
2. Close to death

3. Permanently unconscious
4. Advanced progressive illness
5. Extraordinary suffering

None of these criteria applies to Carl. For this reason we have a sixth timing option:

6. Alzheimer's dementia and certain benchmark events have occurred.

Under the sixth timing option Carl would be able to contract with his Health Care Decision Maker and his doctor while he still had control of his mental faculties. He could then determine that his end-of-life options would go into effect when his Alzheimer's reached a certain stage of progression.

Only the patient may choose ahead of time what that stage of progression is and spell it out in his Contract for Compassionate Care. Carl wanted his curative care to cease when the following circumstances had all come to pass: being bedridden, being unable to care for or feed himself, and not being able to recognize his family and friends for a period of one year.

In other words, Carl Novack would have felt that when all those conditions had come to pass, it no longer made sense to try to prolong his life through curative treatment of possible exit events.

As always, Carl would be given all available medical care designed to provide comfort. He would be offered food and water at regular intervals, including three nutritional meals daily. The food would be set by his bed, but he would not be fed if he couldn't or didn't feed himself. What he would not be given are trips to the hospital to treat infection, medications to keep his heart going for as long as possible, and IV nutrition or fluids when he was no longer able to eat or drink. Possible exit events would not be prevented, and a natural death would be allowed to come sooner rather than later.

Had the Compassion Protocol been available to Carl Novack, he most likely would have experienced a natural death several years before Dr. Fitzpatrick met him in the ER.

STEP ONE SUMMARY

Step One of the Compassion Protocol, then, is all about knowing your options. For most of us, our first option is to fight against death as long as we possibly can, taking advantage of the miracles of modern medicine whenever possible. But we may eventually reach the point where our doctors can keep us alive even though we have lost our ability to live independently, are in intolerable pain, and/or are descending into irreversible dementia.

To summarize, the treatment options we have considered in Step One are these:

1. Don't go to the hospital again.
2. Refuse antibiotics.
3. Discontinue your usual medications.
4. Refuse hydration and nutrition.

But it is not enough to know your treatment options. You must also know the timing options—those triggers whereby your choices will be implemented. These are the timing options:

1. Immediately
2. When you are close to death
3. If you are permanently unconscious
4. If you suffer from advanced progressive illness
5. If you are experiencing extraordinary suffering
6. If you suffer from Alzheimer's dementia and certain benchmark events have occurred—for example, you can no longer feed yourself or recognize your loved ones

Thanks to the Compassion Protocol, you don't have to keep fighting for a life that is no longer preferable to death. When you reach that point, you can consider what options you might employ—and when they should be employed—to make sure a natural death is allowed to occur if that is your choice.

Step One educates you about the choices available to you. In the next chapter you will find a set of tools to employ that will enable you to choose the end-of-life care options you desire.

CHAPTER SEVEN

STEP TWO:
MAKE YOUR DECISIONS

A lthough we know death is unavoidable, most of us push that thought away into the closet of worries that we just don't think about. In any guise, death is unpleasant to consider, and we live in a culture where it is almost socially unacceptable to talk about it. But spending a few hours now while you are well (or at least sentient) can eliminate incalculable amounts of emotional or physical pain and suffering in the future.

INTRODUCTION
TO STEP TWO

In taking the steps of the Compassion Protocol, you may find comfort from knowing that you are not alone: Death is the one certainty each of us must face. But you need not face it unprepared. The Compassion Protocol enables you to think and talk about your own death in a way that can actually decrease anxiety by giving you some measure of choice and control at the end of your life.

Step Two prepares you to make two sets of choices: (1) your option and timing decisions, and (2) your choice of a Health Care Decision Maker. Step Two provides two tools to help you make your choices and determine if the Compassion Protocol is right for you.

If you are at the end of your life and choosing to implement Comfort Care Only immediately, you should complete the Compassion Protocol Worksheet and a Pros and Cons List of factors that will impact your decision. These forms are discussed below, are included in appendix B, and are available on our Web site.

If you are completing the Compassion Protocol proactively while still in good health, these tools will not have current relevance; however, we recommend that you familiarize yourself with them in order to discuss their future application with your Health Care Decision Maker.

THE COMPASSION PROTOCOL WORKSHEET

The Compassion Protocol Worksheet is composed of five questions that may help you make your option and timing decisions. When you are ready to implement Comfort Care Only, these questions will encourage you to search your heart and mind to determine whether the Compassion Protocol is right for you.

1. Am I just depressed?

2. Is it possible life could get better again?

3. Do I have any important unfinished business?

4. Do I still enjoy waking up in the morning?

5. Am I ready to let death happen?

We will look at these questions in more detail and discuss them as they relate to the Compassion Protocol's three eligible groups: the sentient elderly, the terminally ill, and those with Alzheimer's dementia who chose the Compassion Protocol while they were still in control of their faculties.

QUESTION 1: AM I JUST DEPRESSED?

Depression can be defined generally as an inability to enjoy life. As you gradually lose your health, you may become unable to do the things you have always enjoyed doing. You may mourn the activities you've lost, but can you still enjoy a grandchild's visit, a specially baked treat, or a favorite TV program?

Willa Simpson, one of the sentient elderly, would have answered the question about depression in the negative. Drs. Fitzpatrick and Street evaluated her mental status and found it to be normal. They found none of the markers that would have alerted them to depressive tendencies. In fact, Willa was facing her situation with a degree of humor.

The terminally ill, such as Melissa Blackburn, who had metastatic lung cancer, often fight depression valiantly in the face of overwhelming odds but finally reach a point when the suffering endured exceeds the pleasure of living life. Rather than being a marker of depression, such a decision is in keeping with the actions one might take upon realizing the time has come to allow a natural death to occur.

As for Carl Novack, the former university professor suffering end-stage Alzheimer's dementia, he had been unable to communicate any coherent idea or observation for several years. His physical suffering was not difficult to assess as he moaned in pain. Depression as a clinical possibility is more relevant during the early stages of dementia. Those with Alzheimer's dementia who are considering choosing the Compassion Protocol should discuss depression with their doctors before proceeding.

Notice that this first question asks, Am I *just* depressed? Depression is common in the elderly and tends to be undertreated. It is probable that depression is present to some degree in many of those who are considering choosing the Compassion Protocol. Depression is not the primary issue. Looking at all five of our Compassion Protocol Worksheet questions, the key is that a candidate for the Compassion Protocol is not only depressed but would answer questions two, three, and four in the negative.

QUESTION 2: IS IT POSSIBLE LIFE COULD GET BETTER AGAIN?

If it is pain that makes you want to die, all possible improvements in your pain medication should be thoroughly explored. New avenues in relieving pain may make you comfortable a bit longer.

If your illness has isolated you from society, there might be a church group, senior citizens group, or volunteer organization that would again offer you social interaction. If heart or lung disease has crippled you, ask your doctor one more time if there is any other treatment—or perhaps a visit to a specialist—that might make life more endurable.

The worksheet in appendix B actually asks you these questions and gives you space to write your answers. Your doctor then has an opportunity to discuss your answers with you. Willa Simpson, Melissa Blackburn, and Carl Novack would have no trouble answering, "No, it is not possible that my life could get better." They had all exhausted the palliative measures available to them and concluded (or, in Carl's case, his Health Care Decision Maker concluded) that under no circumstances could they envision an improvement in their quality of life.

You need to be sure you have exhausted the possibilities for improving your life before you decide to let it end sooner rather than later.

QUESTION 3: DO I HAVE ANY IMPORTANT UNFINISHED BUSINESS?

This question most often involves repair of damaged relationships. Is there a child, sibling, or parent that you have fought with who might like a chance to make amends with you before you die? Are there people who will feel guilty when you die, and do you want to give them a chance to avoid that guilt? This is also a good time to check your will or trust estate one more time.

The hospice program has been useful in terminal illness cases by providing counseling in family sessions that help facilitate a dialog between the terminally ill patient and his or her friends and family. The question of unfinished business is a critical one to answer before proceeding with plans for your end-of-life strategy.

QUESTION 4: DO I STILL ENJOY WAKING UP IN THE MORNING?

This may be the most important question to consider. If you are approaching death for any reason, you may wonder as you go to sleep: Will I wake up in the morning?

How do you feel when consciousness first dawns in the morning? Do you think, "Hooray, I get one more day!" or "Oh no, I'm still alive." If you are thankful to awaken again, then you are not ready to implement the Contract for Compassionate Care.

QUESTION 5: AM I READY TO LET DEATH HAPPEN?

More specifically, do you want to let death happen in any of the specific, carefully crafted circumstances set forth in Step One? This is a question that you need to discuss with family, close friends, a doctor, and/or a spiritual advisor.

YOUR LIST OF PROS AND CONS

Step Two employs a second decision-making tool: creating a list of the pros and cons of choosing your end-of-life options, such as the following examples.

I want to live because …

… my family will miss me.

… sunrises are still beautiful.

… I want to know what happens next week.

… I'm just not ready to say good-bye.

… I'm still glad to wake up in the morning.

I am ready to let death happen because …

… I'm in horrible pain.

… I can no longer do things I want to do.

… I can't live alone anymore, and I don't want to live in a nursing home.

… I don't want to be a burden to my family.

… I can't take care of my basic needs anymore.

… the pleasure of life no longer outweighs the pain.

Our Pros and Cons Worksheet (appendix B) provides one page for pros or Reasons to Continue Living. Start by taking information from what you wrote on your Compassion Protocol Worksheet. Then consider your life from various perspectives, starting with your everyday routine and also including yearly events such as holidays and family visits. Think about all the people you are in contact with, those you might miss and those who might miss you. Quiet your thoughts and then ask yourself, "What brings me joy? What puts a smile on my face? What makes me happy?"

On the second page of the Pros and Cons Worksheet, list your Reasons to Want a Natural Death to Occur Sooner Rather Than Later. Again, start by gleaning from what you wrote on your Compassion Protocol Worksheet. Consider your life from various perspectives, from daily occurrences to rare occasions. Think about all the people you are in contact with, those you might miss and those who might miss you. Quiet your thoughts and then ask yourself: "What weighs on me? What makes me long for the peace of my final sleep? What aspects of my life have gone beyond unsatisfactory and have become burdensome?"

Your Pros and Cons List will help you identify the reasons you might choose the Compassion Protocol. This list can also be shared with those close to you with whom you will be discussing your choices, whatever they may be.

To better understand how Step Two works to help you with your health care and timing options, let's take a closer look at our Alzheimer's patient, Carl Novack, and consider how his illness would have played out in its earliest stages.

A STORY OF OUR OWN WORST FEARS

Carl Novack first noticed memory problems in his late forties. The first time he had a major memory loss was at a Thanksgiving dinner. The day before, his daughter, Lynn, had called from college. She and Carl had a pleasant chat. She talked about the classes she was taking and about the possibility of getting a tutor for her calculus class. They then made plans for Carl to pick her up the next day at her college, which was about an hour away. Carl said he'd be there at 10 a.m.

Carl got up early on Thanksgiving and went to his office. He was working under a deadline for a journal article he was writing and was going to get a few hours of work in before picking Lynn up from college.

At eleven Lynn called home. "What happened to Dad?" she asked. Her mom, Laurel, said she would try him at his office. Something must have come up.

Laurel called Carl at his office. He answered cheerfully. When Laurel asked him why he hadn't gone to pick up Lynn yet, Carl had no idea what she was talking about. He had no memory whatsoever of his conversation with Lynn the previous day or of the plans they had made.

Carl had difficulty accepting that events which happened during his memory lapse really did happen. Yet they must have. As Carl considered the incident, he had an uneasy feeling in his stomach. How could this have occurred?

Carl and Laurel passed the memory lapse off as just one of those things. Carl was probably stressed out and overtired from working on his journal article. There was nothing they could do.

Carl decided to ask for an extension on the article and resolved not to work so hard. Life went on.

But this episode was the beginning of a series of occasional but similar lapses that gradually evolved into increasingly more forgetful behavior. Carl chose to ignore the problem, and Laurel covered for him as often as possible, functioning as a surrogate memory for Carl whenever she could. More than two years passed before Carl saw his doctor and admitted what was happening. Carl was fifty-two when he was diagnosed with Alzheimer's dementia.

Alzheimer's dementia is our worst fear. As we pass through middle age, a faint voice whispers in our ear whenever our memory is less than perfect: Does one become more forgetful as a normal part of the aging process, or could it be Alzheimer's?

Dr. Fitzpatrick likes to describe the distinction between Alzheimer's and normal forgetfulness by saying, "If you forget where you put your glasses, that's everyday forgetfulness. If you forget you *wear* glasses, that may be Alzheimer's." People with normal forgetfulness—which definitely increases with age—are aware of their lapses. People with early Alzheimer's usually don't know their memory is developing holes.

The Compassion Protocol is specifically tailored to give help to people in the early stages of Alzheimer's. Let's see what would have happened had Carl been able to follow the Compassion Protocol.

STEP TWO AND THE ALZHEIMER'S PATIENT

In this scenario, Carl encounters the Compassion Protocol while still in the early stages of his disease. He has recently had his worst fears confirmed—he has Alzheimer's dementia. He has done his research and knows enough about what the future holds to want to proactively choose his own end-of-life care.

Carl can use the Compassion Protocol to learn what his options are. He might decide to use all four options to allow a natural death:

- Don't go to the hospital again.
- Refuse antibiotics.
- Discontinue your usual medications.
- Refuse hydration and nutrition.

For the Alzheimer's patient, the fourth option can be extended to mean "Let me eat and drink only by choice." Food and water can be offered to him, but when he forgets to eat, he will not be reminded, and no one will force food or water on him.

Carl is still enjoying life with his early Alzheimer's, but he knows a time will come when he would rather die of natural causes than continue to lose his mind slowly. He chooses benchmark events that will trigger his withdrawal from curative care:

- No longer able to eat or drink on his own
- No longer able to get to the bathroom on his own
- Unable to recognize family members for a period of one year

Carl notes his timing choices in his Contract for Compassionate Care, but it is even more important that his Health Care

Decision Maker know both his specific choices and the sense of what Carl means by them concerning when he would like to be done with his life as an Alzheimer's patient.

You will find each of the available options listed in Part I of the Contract for Compassionate Care (found in appendix A or downloadable from our Web site). You may choose as few or as many of the end-of-life options as you want: The point is that you are proactively taking control of your own end-of-life care.

Once you have made your option and timing choices, one other important Step Two decision remains.

SELECTING A HEALTH CARE DECISION MAKER

For people who are no longer mentally competent, the decision to implement any or all of the Compassion Protocol options will be made by their designated Health Care Decision Maker. Specifically, in the case of those with early Alzheimer's dementia, we rely on our Health Care Decision Makers to put our end-of-life options into effect when we are no longer able to choose for ourselves.

The long, slow decline from Alzheimer's dementia is one of the worst fears of the baby boomer generation. Choosing the Compassion Protocol can only be accomplished by careful planning while one is still mentally competent.

Without a doubt the most important decision you will ever make regarding your end-of-life care is who will be your Health

Care Decision Maker. Ideally, this should be the person who knows you the best and whom you trust the most—literally, someone you would trust with your life.

Your Health Care Decision Maker should know what you want the end of your life to be like. Perhaps you don't want to be kept alive on a respirator or with a feeding tube, but other than that, you want to continue to live your years for their longest medically sustained duration. Or maybe, like us, you tend more toward choosing all the options and don't want to continue life indefinitely once cognition has gone.

It is vitally important for you and your Health Care Decision Maker to have numerous conversations about your end-of-life options and when they should be implemented. The paths of death are rarely linear, and you will benefit more by talking from the general to the specific and exploring values as well as hypotheticals.

As you will see in chapter 9, Step Four: Do the Paperwork, your Health Care Decision Maker plays a conspicuous role in the signing of your paperwork. This person will be asked a series of questions to be answered for the record in order to document his or her understanding of your end-of-life choices.

The important thing, therefore, is for your Health Care Decision Maker to really know you and what you would want in specific circumstances and for you to be able to trust this person to implement your wishes.

Of course, you will have forms filled out that specify what you want (see appendix A). However, as we explain in chapter 9, the most carefully crafted legal forms are, in the end, only that—legal forms. They can't take the place of human connections with people who know your desires and are ready to fight to implement them.

In our experience, children have the hardest time letting elderly parents die. Perhaps daughters who have cared for their own helpless infants are less overwhelmed by caring for a totally dependent parent. In any case, before designating a daughter or son as your Health Care Decision Maker, you must be sure the person you choose will respect your wishes and let you die even if it goes against his or her own choices. If there is no family member you can trust with your end-of-life decisions, you may need to seek a friend who will be your decision maker. Whomever you choose, your Health Care Decision Maker must know your wishes fully and be willing to follow them.

REVIEW

To review, in Step One we described the four treatment options for end-of-life care:

1. Don't go to the hospital again.
2. Refuse antibiotics.
3. Discontinue your usual medications.
4. Refuse hydration and nutrition.

In Step Two we presented two important sets of decisions. First, you may choose to exercise some or all of the options for a natural death under certain circumstances. Second, you designate a family member or trusted friend to act as your Health Care Decision Maker.

As we have seen, Step Two provides two tools to help in making your option decisions:

1. Working through the Compassion Protocol Worksheet, in which you ask yourself these five important questions:
    i.   *Am I just depressed?*
    ii. *Is it possible that life could get better again?*
    iii. *Do I have any important unfinished business?*
    iv. *Do I still enjoy waking up in the morning?*
    v.   *Am I ready to let death happen?*
2. Making a Pros and Cons List for choosing the Compassion Protocol to increase choice and control at the end of life.

If you are mentally competent, you will decide for yourself when to exercise the options you've chosen. If you are not competent, you will be relying on your Health Care Decision Maker to know when you want to be allowed a natural death.

This requires a relationship of trust and confidence. It is difficult—if not impossible—to spell out every possibility for when your Step One options will come into play. Rather than trying to delineate every possible end-of-life scenario, you must express in broad terms your end-of-life philosophy and how you expect your wishes to be followed. Ideally, you should know that your designated decision maker will be able to make difficult decisions about your care in line with your wishes.

With your choice of a Health Care Decision Maker, you have completed your Step Two choices:

1. Making your end-of-life options and timing decisions; and
2. Selecting a Health Care Decision Maker.

By the end of the Step Two process you will have a better understanding about how you want your end-of-life experience to unfold. You will have made the decisions necessary to implement increased choice and control in your final days. It is now time to communicate your decisions.

CHAPTER EIGHT

STEP THREE: COMMUNICATE YOUR DECISIONS

Our culture simply doesn't talk about dying. Although the taboo has lifted somewhat over the past twenty years thanks to groups such as the Project on Death in America and Compassionate Dying, talking about death and dying is still difficult.

Nonetheless, if you decide you want to choose the Compassion Protocol for your end-of-life care, you must communicate your decision to your doctor and other health care providers, your Health Care Decision Maker, your family, your next of kin, and a close friend or two—that is, to the community of people who care for you and who will advocate for your decisions to be carried out if you become incapacitated.

Whether you are already in end-of-life circumstances and you want to implement some of your options now or are planning ahead for the future, your goal is the same. Everyone involved in your care needs to know that you have decided you want to let natural death occur if clearly delineated events transpire. It is very important that *everyone* who spends time with you knows your wishes.

Step Three is all about communication. To review:

Step One: Know your options.
Step Two: Make your decisions.
Step Three: Communicate your decisions.
Step Four: Do the paperwork.
Step Five: Plan the kind of death you want.

At this point you have considered your end-of-life options. You have considered or completed the Compassion Protocol Worksheet and chosen your Health Care Decision Maker. But all the good work you have done up to this point will count as nothing if you do not adequately communicate your decisions.

Dr. Fitzpatrick shares the experience of Ray Sullivan to illustrate what happens when Step Three communication fails.

THE IMPORTANCE OF FULL AND ADEQUATE COMMUNICATION: THE STORY OF RAY SULLIVAN

William Barrett and his sister, Joy, a registered nurse, provide residential care in their home for up to three individuals. Their clients are the elderly or disabled who are not able to live alone and need care available 24/7. One of their clients, Ray Sullivan, came to them after he suffered a small stroke. Ray's mind was not affected, but he experienced paralysis on the right side of his body.

Ray was sixty-two years old and came from a large close-knit family. He had never married or had children but was close to his three siblings and their children, now in their early thirties. Six of his nieces and nephews lived locally. Ray was a favorite uncle and was very involved in their lives.

Ray and his family felt he would benefit from his time at the Barretts' home. It was Ray's hope and the hope of his family that he would regain sufficient strength and movement to return to his own home and live independently. A physical therapist came to work with Ray three times a week. Unfortunately, into his third week at the Barretts' Ray suffered another stroke, far more serious this time, robbing him of speech and possibly cognition. It was hard to tell.

He was in the hospital for ten days. Joy Barrett visited him there and talked to his family extensively. Ray was awake but failed to respond to the simplest questions. His family told Joy that it had been Ray's wish never to go into a nursing home, and the family had the resources to pay for private care such as he would receive at Joy's home. The family continued to hope that with regular physical and occupational therapy his condition would improve.

After three months of intensive work with his therapists, Ray's condition was unchanged. He had periods of sleep and wakefulness. He ate food when spoon-fed and drank the liquids offered to him. But he continued to neither speak nor show any interest in what others said or did. William Barrett bathed him every morning and settled him into a wheelchair, where he would spend the day, staring blankly straight ahead.

Ray was into his fourth month at the Barretts' when he woke up during the night moaning loudly. Joy took his temperature and checked his vital signs. His lungs sounded occluded, and Joy suspected pneumonia. She called Ray's brother Paul, explained the situation, and said she would call for an ambulance and that Paul could meet Joy and Ray at the hospital.

Paul asked her to hold off on calling the ambulance until he arrived at the Barretts'. He came within the hour accompanied by his sister and two of his own grown children. They gathered around Ray's bed, stroked his forehead, held his hands, and talked to him. As had been the case during the past three months, Ray was unresponsive to any and all of the attentions of his family.

Paul asked Joy if they could all gather in the living room and discuss the situation. It was three in the morning. Paul acted as spokesman for all the Sullivans. He asked Joy what would happen to Ray if they did not take him to the hospital. Joy said she strongly suspected Ray had pneumonia, and if it was left untreated, he would probably die within a week. There was silence in the room as the Sullivans exchanged glances.

Paul told Joy and her brother that Ray had made it clear to all of them that he would never want to live if he became unable to care for himself. After his first stroke, Ray was determined to work hard at regaining his independence. But it was clearly on his mind that should he become completely incapacitated, he would not want to continue living once his mind was gone. Paul asked Joy to keep Ray comfortable here in her home and not call for ambulance transport to the hospital to cure the pneumonia.

At this point Joy felt she faced a horrendous decision. Ray had never spoken to her about his feeling that he didn't want to be kept alive if he lost all mental and physical functioning. His family wanted to let Ray die. Could she take their word for it? They seemed like caring people who only wanted what Ray had expressed as his desires at the end of life. If she followed their wishes, she would have to trust that they were acting out of the purest of motives.

Meanwhile, Joy felt she had a legal and ethical duty to provide curative care to Ray. She also felt that her duty conflicted with the wishes of Ray's family. She had no way of knowing independently what Ray would have wanted. In the absence of clear direction from Ray, she felt she should err on the side of caution. She reluctantly told Ray's family that she would call for the ambulance and let the ER doctors decide what level of care Ray should receive.

Ray's family was distraught. They continued to argue with Joy and her brother even as Joy was phoning for the ambulance. They threatened a lawsuit. Joy felt she was far more likely to face liability if she chose not to act than if she did. She felt her duty was clear: At best she had to treat Ray's pneumonia, and at the least she had to let the ER doctors evaluate his condition.

To avoid this unhappy outcome, all Ray had to do was talk to his caregivers (Joy and her brother) about his wishes. In the absence of written Advance Directives, Ray's oral expression of his end-of-life wishes may have been sufficient to meet the "clear and convincing evidence" standard for the expression of his wishes.

Joy did call for the ambulance. When it arrived, the EMT personnel strapped Ray to a gurney and drove him to the local hospital. Despite the protestations of Ray's family, the ER doc started Ray on IV antibiotics and admitted him to the hospital.

Ray was in the hospital for five days, and his pneumonia was fully treated. Afterward he went to the home of one of his sisters, where he received round-the-clock nursing care. He died of an untreated urinary tract infection eight months later.

WHAT CONSTITUTES EFFECTIVE COMMUNICATION?

The Compassion Protocol is a communication-dependent program of action. In Step Four you will complete the Contract for Compassionate Care, paperwork that will greatly increase the odds that your end-of-life wishes will be carried out.

But the proper paperwork constitutes only a part of effective communication of your wishes, and it should represent a condensed version of the conversations you have held with all those who have an interest in your well-being and care. Communicating your wishes orally is sufficient to let people know, clearly and convincingly, what your wishes are. With proper verbal communication, those wishes should be as strictly enforced as if you wrote them out at length. That is why we encounter Step Three: Communicate Your Decision prior to Step Four: Do the Paperwork.

It doesn't matter if you are twenty-five or ninety-five. The time to do this is now. If you are young and healthy, you need at least to share your decisions with your Health Care Decision Maker and your closest loved ones who would be most deeply impacted by your death. A few hours today, while you are still healthy or at least mentally competent, may help you avoid months or years of unnecessary suffering.

We will consider here all the available people to whom you should communicate your decisions.

TELL YOUR HEALTH CARE
DECISION MAKER

Whether you are young and healthy and proactively choosing end-of-life options to be used later or you are facing the end of life and implementing the decision you have made using the Compassion Protocol immediately, it is critically important that your Health Care Decision Maker knows your wishes. Your Health Care Decision Maker should clearly understand what medical treatment options you would choose and under what circumstances.

TELL YOUR DOCTOR AND OTHER
HEALTH CARE PROVIDERS

For the young and healthy who are planning proactively: Bring your Contract for Compassionate Care to your next physical, explain your wishes to your doctor, and have him or her sign the contract. Then file it away and go on with the business of living, secure in the knowledge that should disaster strike, you have clearly communicated your wishes for the end of your life.

If you are at the end of your life and beginning the implementation of the care choices you developed using the Compassion Protocol, you must communicate your decision to all the doctors and other health care providers involved in your care. Make an appointment with your doctor for the purpose of discussing end-of-life care. When the receptionist asks you why you are seeing the doctor, tell her you want to review your end-of-life care decisions with the doctor.

When you meet with your doctor, tell her or him that after lots of careful thought you have decided that you would like the option of a natural death as part of your end-of-life care, and you want your doctor to agree to let you find one. Take your paperwork with you and go with your doctor through your decision-making process and your choices carefully.

If you (or your Health Care Decision Maker) decide you want to implement some of your options right away, your doctor should be willing to assist you. He or she may, for example, write orders for discontinuing some of your medications, sign your Contract for Compassionate Care, and forward it to your nursing home or to your home health caregivers.

If you are already chronically ill and at the end of life, your doctor should also help you get signed up with a hospice for your end-of-life care. The hospice will provide you with all available comfort measures as you approach death. (This is discussed in more detail in chapter 11.)

Most important, if your doctor refuses to honor your decision, find a doctor who will. You have the right to determine your end-of-life medical treatment.

If you are the caregiver and/or Health Care Decision Maker for someone unable to communicate his or her wishes, it will be your task to tell the doctors when your loved one wants Comfort Care Only and when withdrawal from curative care is to be implemented. You must feel confident that, as your loved one's legal representative, you have the right and duty to make sure his or her end-of-life wishes are followed by the health care system. If the Compassion Protocol was completed before you were appointed the Health Care Decision Maker, your job will be much easier.

TELL YOUR FAMILY

For those who are planning ahead, it is also a good idea to share your wishes with other loved ones and relatives who may become involved in your end-of-life care. If you feel that certain family members might have very different views on the end of life and might fight your decision, tell them yourself about the decisions you have made. In general, for the young and healthy, just talking to your Health Care Decision Maker is sufficient. Once you have had those critical conversations, you can put your contract away and get on with living.

If you are approaching the end of life, those who have watched you suffer the pain, loss, and indignity of chronic illness should be told next. The hope is that they will understand and respect your decision.

Those you tell may respond at first with denial. A typical response is that of Dr. Hastings to Phyllis Shattuck in chapter 1: "Now, Phyllis, you're not going to die. Don't be silly." The best response to denial is "You're the one who's being silly. Of course

I'm dying [or: Of course I'm going to die eventually]—everybody dies. I just want a little control about how and when I do it."

At the point when you are sharing your end-of-life choices, you will have completed the Compassion Protocol Worksheet. Use this worksheet as a template for explaining why you have made the choices you have. Sharing the insights you gained from Step Two will help your family understand your choices. The completed worksheet will help people around you know that this is not an impetuous or sudden decision but is one that you came to slowly and thoughtfully. Ask your loved ones to read this book, with its stories of the kind of death you want to avoid.

If you run into a brick wall of resistance, seek a mediator. Professional health care mediators are trained to bring people together over difficult problems arising out of terminal illness and death. A hospice or a local hospital may be able to help you find one.

TELL YOUR FRIENDS

If you are young and healthy, there is no urgent need to discuss your end-of-life choices with your friends. But you might consider talking to them about your choices as a kindness, to inspire them to consider their own wishes and make similar proactive arrangements.

Once you have reached the end of life and have chosen to receive Comfort Care Only, and your decision has been accepted by your family, your doctors, and your caregivers, you should let your friends know. At the appropriate time they will have an opportunity to say good-bye to you, and vice versa.

By completing Step Three you have moved death out of the closet and into the open. Death is a natural part of life. By sharing your acceptance you do a service to yourself, your family, and your friends.

DR. FITZPATRICK TALKS ABOUT HER END-OF-LIFE CHOICES

My Health Care Decision Maker knows my wishes already. I have done the paperwork to make sure she can carry out my wishes. The paperwork allows her to choose all four of the options listed in Step One if I am unable to choose them myself.

My Health Care Decision Maker knows that if for any reason I become *permanently* unable to make rational decisions or communicate them, she is directed to assume that I am ready to die. I have told her, "If for *any* reason I am unable to tell you what I want, assume that on the inside I am screaming at you, 'Please let me die.'"

If I begin the long, slow decline into dementia due to Alzheimer's, my Decision Maker will exercise the first three options for me as soon as I am no longer able to coherently and consistently answer the five questions listed in Step Two of the Compassion Protocol.

Even fairly early in Alzheimer's, while I am still able to carry on coherent conversations at times and still recognize family most of the time, my Health Care Decision Maker will let me take advantage of any possible exit event and die a natural death—without a trip to the hospital for pneumonia or other curable illness.

Yes, I am giving my Health Care Decision Maker a lot of leeway and power over my life, but she knows full well that I do not want to live when my mind no longer works. And even if it is very difficult for her, I want her to be especially careful not to rob me of an exit event early in dementia that could save me from a year or two (or five or ten) in a nursing home or at home when I would be a burden to my family.

My decision maker will let me exercise the fourth end-of-life option, refusing food and water, naturally as the disease progresses. For example, if I stop asking to eat or drink, she won't remind me to do so. She will place food and water by my bedside three times daily, but without interference she will let me freely decide whether to eat or drink.

ATTORNEY FITZPATRICK TALKS ABOUT HER END-OF-LIFE CHOICES

As of this writing, I am a fifty-seven-year-old mother of three grown children. It is noteworthy—though not outside the norm—that I find the subject matter of this book difficult to discuss with my kids. This hesitancy is on a par with the shocking fact that many of my friends and colleagues have made no provision for incapacitating illness or death, not even executing a simple will or trust instrument.

One of the societal benefits of our book is to provide a framework through which this important topic may be broached. My Health Care Decision Maker is one of my children, the one who is geographically closest to where I live. She and I have spent many hours describing how I want my final years to be and when to "pull the plug."

I believe our thoughts about death and how we want our own death to play out are informed by two sets of circumstances: first, by how our family treated the death of loved ones while we were growing up, and second, by any hands-on experience we have had observing someone die.

My family tends to think that life is for the living, so when someone dies, you mourn (briefly) and move on. And when you are old and infirm, you surely don't want to inconvenience anyone.

Values we absorb and memories we internalize as we grow up are powerful influences on our approach to our own death. My grandfather suffered from senile dementia for a year or so before he died at the age of eighty-six. I was in high school at the time. The last time I went to see him, six months before he died, I was wholly unprepared for the chilly indifference he exhibited toward me.

The morning after my grandfather died I went to visit my grandmother, who was bedridden in the full care section of the retirement community. She told me that she was awakened at about 11 p.m. the previous night to find Grandfather standing beside her bed. He grasped her arm and told her to get up and come with him right then. It was important.

Grandmother really wanted to go with him, but she had been bedridden for months and just couldn't make her limbs work.

Grandfather had also been bedridden for the better part of a year and hadn't recognized her for longer than that.

When she woke up the next morning, she found out that Grandfather had died the previous evening shortly before eleven. The story is remarkable not because of its content but because *she* told it—a hardheaded Scot who never had a fanciful thought in her life. Also, I believe I am the only family member she told of this experience, either because I was considered religious or, more likely, because I was often open to kooky ideas.

I didn't attend the funerals for either grandparent because there were none. My family doesn't have funerals. I have no idea what happened to their remains because no one in my family ever talks about those kinds of things.

The lessons I learned from these experiences, whether good or bad, is that old age and infirmity bring loss of control. When one descends into dementia, it is as if no one is home. Physical life goes on while emotional or spiritual life has left the body. As for Grandmother's dream, you may think you have a tight grip on intellectual reality even while your subconscious has other plans.

Using the steps of the Compassion Protocol, I have been able to discuss these issues with my Health Care Decision Maker. Of the greatest importance to me is that if I descend into dementia and for six months do not recognize friends or family members, I would like all four Step One options to go into effect. This might seem rather drastic, but I think the effects of dementia on friends and family are drastic. It is a great comfort for me to know that I will not linger for long in the fog of Alzheimer's dementia.

We have also talked about what arrangements to make after

I die. Here I find myself following in the footsteps of my family. I don't want a funeral—certainly nothing in a church. The cheapest pine-box cremation is fine. A party at someone's house might be fun. And I've warned my decision maker that she is the one who gets to hear all about any spiritual flights of fancy, just so she will be prepared.

But there should be little sadness or mourning, since, after all, life is for the living.

STEP THREE SUMMARY

At this point you have completed the first three steps of the Compassion Protocol:

Step One: Know Your Options
Step Two: Make Your Decisions
Step Three: Communicate Your Decisions

The good news is that the hard work of the Compassion Protocol is mostly behind you. Knowing your options, deciding what you want your end-of-life experience to be, and sharing your decisions are inherently difficult tasks in a culture that keeps death and dying hidden away in the closet of unmentionables. If you have completed these difficult steps, congratulations! You have made monumental progress toward increasing your own choice and control at the end of your life.

Two steps remain: filling out the paperwork (Step Four) and planning the death you want (Step Five).

CHAPTER NINE

STEP FOUR:
DO THE PAPERWORK

The legal form you need to effect the choices you make using the Compassion Protocol is called the Contract for Compassionate Care (see appendix A or visit www.compassionprotocol .com). This short, simple form is very similar to Oregon's POLST form, but it contains all the information you will need to enable you or your Health Care Decision Maker to have maximum control over your death. In this chapter we review the contract so you may understand each of its parts.

INTRODUCTION TO THE CONTRACT FOR COMPASSIONATE CARE

When a number of forms are required, problems and delays often occur. In a crisis situation you or your caregivers might forget to bring along the Power of Attorney for Health Care while remembering the Living Will, or some similar error. Valuable time may be wasted while searching for the paperwork. Unless the ambulance crew or the ER doctors actually have your paperwork in hand, they will resuscitate you, work to cure your acute condition, and perform all available heroic measures to prolong your life.

For this reason we have chosen to combine all the necessary legal components of the Compassion Protocol into one single-page document. Presenting everything in one document is the best way to ensure that things go smoothly and all your wishes are honored.

LEGAL BASIS OF THE COMPASSION PROTOCOL

According to the law, Advance Directive forms are valid until proven otherwise. This is very important: If someone wants to challenge the validity or legality of your decision to choose Comfort Care Only, the burden of proof is on them to show that the document is not a valid expression of your choices. The court will assume that your Contract for Compassionate Care was executed by you while you were of sound mind and that it correctly sets forth your legally binding wishes.

Anyone wanting to challenge the validity of your choice has to present evidence in court that proves otherwise. In other words, a challenger must prove that your Contract for Compassionate Care was not executed by you or that you were not of sound mind at the time or that it does not correctly set forth your wishes. Short of such proof, your Contract for Compassionate Care will be enforced and will act as a blueprint for what you want your end-of-life experience to be.

Videotaping the signing of your contract is the best way to establish your competence and therefore the validity of your contract. Questions of soundness of mind or undue influence—or any challenge to your Contract for Compassionate Care—will be insignificant in the face of a visual and auditory record of your making your own choices.

Recruit a friend or family member to operate the camera. (The technology of taping your signing is vastly easier given the ability of cameras and cell phones to create streaming video.) Have your Health Care Decision Maker meet you at your doctor's office for a signing party. Include the people you would like to have as witnesses. Address the camera and explain what you are doing. Reading aloud the various parts of the contract as you initial them will also help. In this way you will literally have the last word as to what your choices are.

We will take a look at each part of the contract that you will complete. You can follow along with the contract in appendix A or print one from our Web site.

I.   **Resuscitation Order:** This brief part is your DNR order in which you can ask not to be brought back to life if you are dead—that is, if you have no pulse or are not breathing. This decision is required as part of the Advance Directive in some states. If you request resuscitation, everything will be done to try to restart your heart and lungs, including shocking your heart, placing you on a pacemaker, or putting a tube into your lungs to connect you to a ventilator. If you request Do Not Resuscitate, your heart will not be restarted, and you will not have a tube passed into your lungs to artificially breathe for you. Signing this part allows your health care provider to disconnect you from artificial life support if it is started before your wishes are known.

II: **Medical Intervention and Timing Order:** These are familiar choices from Step One: Know Your Options and Step Two: Make Your Decisions. This step is where you can choose to withdraw from curative care and allow a natural death to occur without intervention—the heart of the Contract for Compassionate Care. It is very likely that it will be your Health Care Decision Maker, not you, who chooses when this order goes into effect. In the second part you indicate conditions that would cause you to want to withdraw from curative care. It is impossible to imagine all possible conditions, but these will serve as guidelines to empower your Health Care Decision Maker in his or her role of protecting your right to a natural death. As we have emphasized all along, this paperwork is no substitute for the conversation and communication you need to have with your decision maker, doctor, family, and other caregivers.

III: **Appointment of Health Care Decision Maker:** As discussed in chapter 7, this is the single most important work you will do in the Compassion Protocol. While you are still healthy—or at least of sound mind—you will make your own choices. You have the right to choose how you want your end-of-life care to unfold, and you will direct that care. But if you become unable to choose, your Health Care Decision Maker will make your choices for you.

Choosing someone who knows you well and with whom you can discuss your wishes is critically important. You must be comfortable that your decision maker will abide by your wishes when called upon to make some difficult decisions.

At the signing of the Contract for Compassionate Care, ask your Health Care Decision Maker the following questions and record the resulting dialog on your videotape:

1. Are you willing to commit to being my Health Care Decision Maker from today until such time as you decide to step down?
2. What do you consider your responsibilities to be?
3. Can you describe my wishes for end-of-life care?
4. Are you willing to work with my doctors and other health care providers to see that my wishes are carried out even if it requires going against my doctor's advice?
5. Is there anything else you would like to say for the record?

By employing a simple dialog such as this and recording it digitally, you greatly reduce the likelihood that a challenge to your Health Care Decision Maker's choices will succeed. A little proactive effort now can alleviate untold suffering later.

IV. **Signatures:** The Contract for Compassionate Care will be signed by you, your Health Care Decision Maker, two witnesses, and the doctor involved in your care. As discussed above, videotaping the signing is strongly recommended.

V. **Review:** Included is room for you and your doctor to indicate that you have reviewed the form and either changed it, completed a new form, or left it unchanged. Regular review is a requirement in some states.

THE LONG AND SHORT OF LEGAL FORMS

Our Contract for Compassionate Care is designed to clearly and unequivocally set forth your desires for your end-of-life care. However, it may require adjustment in order for it to conform to the laws of the state in which you reside. Only an attorney should modify the form to reduce the risk that a change will compromise the enforceability of the contract. The important thing is that your Contract for Compassionate Care clearly and unequivocally sets forth your desires for your end-of-life care.

Despite its legal importance, signing this paperwork and filling out the Compassion Protocol forms is far from the most important part of the process. Legal documents can be critically helpful, but in the end they are just words on paper.

Documents such as our Contract for Compassionate Care outline duties and responsibilities, but no prepared document can cover all the possibilities of real-life events. For this reason paperwork can never take the place of caring individuals whom you know and trust and who know and understand your desires.

Moreover, legal documents can sometimes fail at what they set out to do. About ten years ago Oregon adopted the POLST form (or Physician Orders for Life-Sustaining Treatment), which was supposed to be the patient's declaration that he or she wanted to cease curative care and receive Comfort Care Only. A bright pink form, the POLST is supposed to follow the patient wherever he goes and be posted at the foot of the bed of all nursing home and hospital patients.

At the time of its creation, Oregon's POLST form was a radical step toward giving patients the tools they need to direct their own medical care. Yet despite the unstinting work of a vibrant Right to Die lobby in Oregon, the POLST form has been a disappointment.

In earlier chapters we saw how POLST forms are routinely ignored by nursing homes; in fact, many nursing homes have chosen to interpret the form as requiring a diagnosis from two attending doctors that the patient is terminally ill. Carl Novack had a POLST form requesting Comfort Care Only, but the staff at his nursing home ignored it and called 911 when he choked and stopped breathing. This action was not an accident but was consistent with the nursing home's policy since Carl had no terminal diagnosis.

It is our hope that moving away from multiple forms and toward a Compassion Protocol that centers on communication for the kind of death you want will lead to increased choice and control at the end of life. The strength of the Compassion Protocol rests on its dual base of written and oral communication.

AND NEVER FORGET THE "PEOPLE" PART

At this point you have already chosen to use the Compassion Protocol, told your doctor and loved ones, and finished filling out and signing, with witnesses, your Compassion Protocol form.

If you are young and healthy, or even old and healthy, the heavy work is done. Put the original document in a safe place, give copies to your family, doctors, and local hospitals, and then forget about it. You have lots of good living left to do, and now you will have less anxiety about that future time when you are approaching death.

The paperwork is necessary, but the "people" part of the Compassion Protocol is most important. Maintaining ongoing communication with your friends and family, health care professionals, and Health Care Decision Maker about your end-of-life wishes is at the heart of the Compassion Protocol. Your openness about your decision and your plans will make a vital contribution to ending the "my patients don't die" attitude that unnecessarily extends suffering at the end of life.

CHAPTER TEN

STEP FIVE: PLAN THE KIND
OF DEATH YOU WANT

We now consider what happens when your health deteriorates and you find yourself in one of the sets of circumstances in which the choices you made using the Compassion Protocol may be implemented. The following discussion assumes that you have gone through the Compassion Protocol Worksheet (appendix B) in Step Two; you have decided that you are now ready to die; and you've chosen the options you want to use that allow you to have a natural death.

The seventeenth-century philosopher Thomas Hobbes said, "Life is nasty, brutish and short." One could also concede that death is often nasty, brutish, and protracted. Dying people rarely close their eyes and peacefully drift off to sleep. When one of the critical organs (heart, lungs, brain) fails, the other two continue for some time before the patient is finally still. That "some time" can be terrifying for the unprepared.

Recall Melissa Blackburn's experience in chapter 4. Her family was determined to follow Melissa's wishes and have her die at home. But when Melissa was alone with her two daughters and had a seizure and began bleeding from her mouth, her daughters called 911.

To avoid unexpected events that you find yourself unable to handle on your own, consider the following changes that can occur attendant to death:

- Seizures, with or without tongue biting and bleeding from the mouth
- Choking and asphyxia
- Loosened bowels
- Gasping for breath
- Agitation, crying out, and even screaming

A hospice is most helpful at educating families and caretakers about what to expect in the last minutes of life and makes available to the caretakers the medications that will ease the suffering attendant to death. A hospice should be involved with everyone who has chosen to institute a Compassion Protocol.

After you have initiated the Compassion Protocol, but before the end comes, you have lots of choices to make about what happens during the next days, weeks, or months that you are dying.

PREPARING THE SPACE

Does the room where you will die have all your important things in it? Have you gathered your favorite pictures? Do you like candlelight? Is music soothing and a source of pleasure for you? Is there some physical object from your religion that gives you comfort? Let your family help you prepare your room.

SAYING GOOD-BYE

Your conversation with family and friends will shift now. It is your time, a chance for them to say good-bye to you, to tell you the things they've forgotten to say. They will need your help with this. Like most people, they may not know how to talk about death or how to say good-bye. You can ease them into the kind of conversation they need to have with you by asking questions like the following:

> What's your favorite memory of things we did
>   together?
> When do you think you'll miss me most?
> How will you remember me?

You can agree that they will stop and remember you at a specific time, such as your birthday or anniversary or when you are in a memorable spot, such as your special place in the park or the hill where you watched sunsets together. You can promise to try to meet again if your religion is one that offers hope beyond death.

LEAVING YOUR LEGACY

This is also the time to distribute your most precious possessions. When families fight after death, it is more often over stuff than over money. Who gets your china is up to you, and your decision is easier for others to accept while you are still alive than after you are dead.

Embracing a Healing Opportunity

Death can be transformative for the living as well as for the dying. You have a chance to heal rifts between family members who will find themselves united in a unique way by your dying. You will give many who visit you a chance to look at their own lives, to decide what is really important, and to let the small stuff slide.

CHANGING SOCIETY ONE DEATH AT A TIME

We strongly believe that our society's fear of and avoidance of death is causing untold suffering both for the dying and for their families. Our Compassion Protocol is the tool we developed to heal the impasse between Do No Harm and Please Let Me Die.

The five simple steps of the Compassion Protocol are designed to help you through the process of facing death so that, as your death approaches, you are an active participant and not a passive victim.

We hope that within a few years the Compassion Protocol will become as accepted a tool for directing events at the end of life as the Advance Directive is currently. With proper planning and careful use of the Compassion Protocol, people will achieve greater choice and control over their end-of-life care.

Our book concludes with a discussion of two essential components of end-of-life care in the United States: hospice, which brings its aid and comfort to the dying, and nursing homes, where millions of the elderly are living out their last days.

CHAPTER ELEVEN

HOSPICE AND THE COMPASSION PROTOCOL

Most people have some familiarity with hospice care, and there are many excellent books on the subject. Hospice, since its beginnings in the 1970s, has eased the pain and suffering of the terminally ill and helped people die with comfort in their own homes. Our purpose is to show how hospice can work in concert with the Compassion Protocol to provide comfort, choice, and control during the most painful and challenging end-of-life circumstances.

THE IMPORTANCE OF FIGHTING FOR LIFE AND OF LETTING GO: DR. FITZPATRICK TELLS THE STORY OF ONE PATIENT'S EXPERIENCE WITH HOSPICE

I met Paul Saxton only three times in his life. The first time was on the day I referred him for hospice care. But on that day I felt I knew him well already: His wife, Alice, had been my patient for about six months when I treated her for depression during her husband's final illness.

Alice was fifty-nine years old, and her husband was two years older. They had been high school sweethearts, each other's first and only love, and married for thirty-nine years. They had three children, all grown and living in other states. Alice's sister, Peggy, lived next door to them on property that had been in the family for years. Peggy always accompanied Alice on her visits to me. Alice would usually give me some physical symptoms—headache, pains in her chest, nausea and vomiting, unable to sleep—and then Peggy would tell me what was going on with Paul.

The first time I saw Alice, she started by telling me that she hadn't slept for a week because of a stomachache that was keeping her up. She couldn't eat, and food just made her nauseous. I asked her all the usual abdominal pain questions: Where does it hurt? Is it crampy or steady? What happens when you eat? What makes it worse? What makes it better? When does it bother you the most? Have you lost weight? Have you had any changes in your bowel habits? She answered them calmly, with good eye contact and normal affect. I was thinking it was a possible ulcer and probably not gallbladder. I was also thinking about what tests to order. It was our first visit together, so I moved on to questions about her medical history (negative except for childbirths) and her family. She told me about her three children and four grandchildren, and then I asked, "Are you still married?"

Her mouth opened and closed a few times, trying to get words out, but instead she crumbled into sobs. Her sister picked up the story, telling me about Paul's colon cancer, which had dominated their lives for the three years since his diagnosis, with surgery followed by the terror of aggressive chemotherapy, brief remission, and another bout of chemo. Paul's colon cancer had just recurred for the third time. He had widely metastatic disease throughout his abdomen and liver. His doctor recommended another round of chemotherapy. Alice sat quietly, head bowed and shoulders hunched inward, looking down at her tightly clenched fists, while Peggy told me the story—how they had just returned to a "normal" life again after the last bout of chemo, with only a four-month break. Alice was back at work, in the office at the Oregon State Parks headquarters where she had worked for thirty-five years. She loved her work, but now she would have to quit again to take Paul to his appointments at the hospital, a forty-five-minute drive from their remote mountain home.

When Peggy finished talking, I sat silently until Alice looked up. Then I said, "It seems very likely that your stomachache is caused by the fact that your husband is dying."

She sat up straight, took a deep breath, and said in a loud, firm voice, "He's not dying. He's going to beat this and get better. This is just a little speed bump, not a roadblock."

From what Peggy had told me, I was fairly certain Paul was going to die from his cancer, probably within a few months. Although her husband had been fighting a terminal disease for three years, Alice was still firmly locked in the early stage of denial.

I made no progress breaking through her denial on that first visit. When I pushed gently against it, she started to get up and walk out. I decided to address her somatic complaints first to try to establish some trust. After an exam and talking about some tests for her stomachache, I asked her if she thought she might be depressed by all the changes in her life. She was able to agree to this, and I started her on an antidepressant. I asked her to return in two weeks to review her tests.

I saw Alice every two to four weeks for the next six months. On each visit we would address her somatic complaints and review her tests, all of which were negative. She got very little relief from the antidepressant. Her insomnia was cured by extreme exhaustion from her constant care of Paul. Each visit Peggy would give me the update on Paul's progress. He received only three months of chemo; he was forced to stop when his liver completely shut down. He developed ascites, massive swelling of the belly from fluid leaking out of the bowel because of the buildup of pressure behind the nonfunctioning liver. I talked to his doctors at the nearby university where he had been receiving his treatment. They told me they had nothing else to offer him, but they hadn't suggested hospice because they knew he hadn't accepted his death. They continued to see him every month and monitored his liver function, drained his ascitic fluid when necessary, and gave him prescriptions for pain medications. They gave him very little chance of a six-month survival but said that he continued to have hope, and they were unwilling to deprive him of that hope.

On each visit I gave Alice at least one opening to talk about Paul's death. I asked her about her own philosophy or religion and her feelings about death. She would talk in the abstract about death and dying but then would continue to insist that Paul wasn't going to die. I always made a point of telling her that help was available whenever she needed it, and I gave her some pamphlets from the local hospice group.

INTRODUCTION TO HOSPICE

Hospice as a concept is rooted in the centuries-old idea of offering shelter and rest, or "hospitality," to weary and sick travelers on a long journey. In the late 1960s the term *hospice* first came to be applied to specialized care for dying patients. During the AIDS era of the 1980s and 1990s, when many young people died tragic deaths, hospice grew rapidly, utilizing mostly volunteer staff and community-based fund-raising. In the past ten years the growth of the movement has accelerated with the availability of both private and public insurance payments and the emergence of for-profit hospice programs.

The hospice program provides comfort and support for people who are terminally ill. Rather than trying to cure an illness, hospice care is provided to make the patient comfortable, ease pain, and help the terminally ill live out the time they have remaining to the fullest extent possible. Nurses visit the home regularly to teach the family to manage the patient's pain and to make medications available. It is usually a requirement for enrollment in hospice that curative treatments be ceased and that the family accept the imminence of death.

The modern hospice philosophy accepts death as the final stage of life. The goal of hospice is to enable patients to continue an alert, pain-free life to the greatest extent possible, and to manage other symptoms so that their last days may be spent with dignity and quality, surrounded by their loved ones.

Hospice services may be provided in the home, in nursing homes or hospitals, or in special hospice care facilities. The most common venue—more than 90 percent of hospice care—is the patient's own home. In many ways the Compassion Protocol is closely allied with hospice care, sharing the same principles of accepting death as the final stage of life and of providing comfort rather than curative care during life's final stages.

As of this writing, more than six hundred thousand patients are enrolled in hospice care on any given day. The average length of stay is about six weeks. The most common primary diagnosis is cancer, but other terminal illnesses are treated as well.

Unfortunately, hospice care is readily available only to the terminally ill. To be referred for hospice care a person must generally have less than six months to live. The person must also want to stop all curative care. Melissa Blackburn, with end-stage cancer, was a typical candidate for hospice care. Willa Simpson and Carl Novack might have had difficulty qualifying. Willa was elderly and beginning to lose her grasp on life but was not terminally ill. Similarly, while Carl Novack had advanced Alzheimer's dementia, he did not suffer from a terminal illness but from the effects of his disease's slow and inevitable progression.

I knew that hospice could bring Paul much needed comfort as his pain escalated rapidly. I also knew it could give Alice the relief that comes from acceptance and support as death approaches. I wasn't at all sure that Paul and Alice would find the hospice information helpful because they were in such denial concerning Paul's illness. But I felt that introducing them to the idea could hardly make things worse.

Difficulty Accepting Death
Even When It Is Imminent

Alice brought the pamphlets with her on her next visit and returned them to me, saying, "This is only for people with a terminal illness who have given up on life. Paul isn't ready to quit his treatment and just give up and die."

"Is he having much pain?" I asked.

Alice closed down, a reaction I had become used to; her body language change always reminded me of a turtle disappearing into its shell.

As usual, Peggy answered for her: "He's in horrible pain all the time. He has some pills for the pain, but they make him nauseated and don't really work much anyway. I wish you could see him. Heck, I wish Alice would really look at him! His eyes are just hollow holes of pain. He looks as if his skin hurts him. I know he doesn't have to suffer so, but they're just so stubborn."

Peggy's eyes teared up in an unusual expression of emotion. She was very good in her role as the strong older sister.

"Alice, do you think his suffering is making him better?" I asked.

For once Peggy remained quiet, and we sat in a silence that stretched on a while.

I finally asked, "Wouldn't you like to see him be comfortable for the time he has left? Wouldn't you like to be able to say goodbye to him and talk about the life you've shared and what life will be like without him?"

Alice sighed, looked around the room, and stretched—definitely a turtle coming back out of its shell. "He's still not ready to give up. I can't ask him to do that if he doesn't want to." In the six months I had known her, this was the closest Alice had come to accepting his imminent death.

I asked her, "Did he look at the information on hospice?"

"No. I tried twice to give it to him, but he just closed his eyes and pretended to be asleep. I got the message. He just can't bear to think about or talk about dying."

"Do you think it might be easier for him to talk to someone else? I'd be happy to come out and talk to him if you think it might help."

"I don't know. I just don't know." The turtle was withdrawing again, and she started to cry.

Peggy put her arm around her sister and said to me, "We've told him a lot about you, and he knows how much help you've been to Alice." This was news to me. I always felt frustrated at my inability to help Alice in any real way. Maybe she was obtaining some relief just from getting out of the house and having someone to talk to.

Peggy continued: "That's a very generous offer." She turned toward her sister and put her hand under her chin to lift Alice's face so they looked at each other from only six inches apart. She leaned forward and rested her forehead on Alice's. "Honey, I'll tell him if you won't. I think he's ready but just doesn't know how to do it. I bet he'll be ready to hear what Dr. Fitzpatrick has to say."

HONESTY, THE BEST POLICY

They called three days later, and I drove out to their home after clinic that day. They lived "up canyon" from the town where I worked, in a stately old farmhouse on sixty acres on a bluff above the river. Peggy, who had never married, lived in an outbuilding that looked well tended and freshly remodeled.

Peggy met me at the door. She said Paul was having a good day. He had been awake for several hours and actually took some soup and a can of Ensure. She led me into the living room, where Paul lay on a twin bed next to double doors leading out to a patio, giving an expansive view of the river and the canyon. Alice sat in a chair pulled up close to the bed.

Paul had a round bald head with a thin layer of skin stretched tight over it and no subcutaneous fat. His eyes were sunken deep into the hollows of pain that Peggy had described. Alice was stroking his arm, which was nothing but skin and bones. Under the thin cover, his distended abdomen, swollen again with ascites, was visible. His breathing was very shallow, compromised by the distended belly. He was the orange-yellow color of end-stage liver failure. His head barely turned to me, but his eyes examined me carefully, and a smile pulled at his mouth.

Peggy introduced me, and Paul said, "Thanks, Doc, for all the help you've been to Alice. Did you come out here to make me all better?" No turtle here. He had an open and easy demeanor that was a surprise to me. I had expected another closed and uncommunicative person like Alice. I decided to just jump right in.

"No, I came out here to talk to you about dying and try to make it a little easier for you. Alice and Peggy seem to think you're a little uncomfortable with the subject."

"Are you used to finding people who want to talk about dying?"

"What we want and what we need aren't always the same

thing. You need to talk about your death, at least that's my opinion, before you can't anymore. You certainly know you're not
going to get any better. I think it would be generous of you to give
Alice a chance to say good-bye. And you look as if you're miserable and could use some help with getting comfortable for your
last days. That's what I came out here to talk to you about."

Now he really grinned and turned to Alice to say, "You're
right—she's a pretty straight talker."

Alice said, "She can help you. I know she can."

"How? She can't cure me. That's the only help I want." His
gaze was locked on Alice's eyes.

There was another chair near the foot of the bed next to Alice's, probably where Peggy usually sat. I pulled it around so that
it faced Paul more directly and sat down. I decided to push on. I
didn't think I could make things any worse by pushing a bit
more.

"You're right, I can't cure the disease that's killing your body.
But how about your heart and soul? Are they as healthy as they
could be at this point? Do you think they might benefit from a
little cleansing honesty and frank talk? And don't you think your
family and friends might like to be invited in to say good-bye?" I
knew from Peggy that Paul had told his children not to visit. He
didn't want them to see him in his wasted condition.

Paul closed his eyes. Alice put her head on the pillow next to
his and said in a barely audible voice, "Please, Paul. She's right—
this could be a little bit easier for all of us."

After some silence Paul started to talk. It was as though a
dam had broken: Thoughts that he had been storing up came
pouring out. He talked for about half an hour without pausing

for comment or interruption. He told me about meeting Alice and falling in love, about moving onto her family's farm when they got married, about each of their children, and about working in the woods for nearly forty years. He said he had done his best to be a good father and husband, and he thought he had been a good person. He said he didn't hate anyone and had always tried to be generous and kind.

"I was raised going to church and pretty much believing in the Creator, though I was never born again or anything like that. Now I just don't know. It doesn't seem likely that there's going to be anything after this life. It just all seems so pointless and sad. How's a person supposed to get his mind around a death like this?"

There were tears in my eyes when he finished, and Peggy, Alice, and Paul were quietly crying. The bit of anger he had had when he began talking had worn itself out. We just sat quietly, all of us gazing out the window.

I broke the silence first: "You're right, Paul. It is sad beyond belief. You're a young man dying before his time. The only antidote I've ever found for that sadness is the love of family and friends. It's your time to accept as much of that love as you can and to let your family give you as much of it as they can. It's easier to do that when you're able to talk about it and share it with them."

After another silence Paul said, "I'm just so tired of the pain. Most days I think the end would be a relief."

Peggy said, "The kids want to come home and say good-bye to you. They all call me to talk because they can't talk to you. They would really like to see you before you die."

Alice finally spoke with a very husky voice: "Let's invite

them home. I know they want to come. You want to see them, don't you?"

They talked a bit about family arrangements. I thought my work was done and got ready to go. Before leaving I told Paul I would have the hospice nurse come out to talk with them and help him as much as possible to deal with the pain so that he could get more pleasure out of visiting with his family. Peggy walked me to the door after Paul and Alice thanked me.

HOSPICE COMFORT AT THE END OF LIFE

I called our local hospice the same day, and Paul and Alice met with the hospice nurse in their own home the very next day. Alice remained my patient and told me about Paul's last days.

All three of the children and all four grandchildren made it home to say good-bye. Hospice brought liquid morphine into the house and showed Alice and Peggy how to give it to Paul. Hospice also gave them other medicines to help with anxiety, insomnia, and nausea. I made another visit two days after the first and did a paracentesis in their living room, draining nearly a gallon of fluid out of his abdomen to ease his breathing and make him more comfortable.

The hospice nurse came every other day. A social worker came to the house to arrange for other services, including physical therapy, counseling, respite care, and even massage. Alice said she wished they had signed up for hospice sooner, that they really could have used some of those things during the miserable three months before the end. It was too late now for most of what hospice had to offer.

Paul asked for more and more of the morphine, resting comfortably for the first time in months. He would let it wear off for part of each day to visit with his family, but he told Alice it was harder and harder to bear the pain. He looked forward more and more to the rest that the morphine brought. During his last two days he didn't really wake up but would moan occasionally and become restless. They would give him the liquid morphine until he was comfortable again. He died a quiet and peaceful death surrounded by his family two weeks after he first availed himself of hospice care.

THE TEAM APPROACH

As Paul and Alice's story reflects, hospice has many services to offer. Managing physical symptoms and providing comfort care in the last days of life are important elements of hospice care, but they are only the beginning. Hospice provides psychological counseling; spiritual counseling; social services and support; help with personal care needs such as bathing, getting dressed, and brushing teeth; help with everyday activities such as running errands and preparing meals; and grief counseling for the patient's loved ones.

The counseling was particularly helpful for Paul, Alice, and their families because they had been putting off accepting Paul's death for so long. They were able to have a family session with the grief counselor, which helped them all make progress in accepting Paul's death.

This kind of team approach is integral to the hospice mission. The patient and the patient's family receive all available services to help them through the death process. If you qualify for hospice care in addition to your personal doctor, you will be working with a team of health care professionals: doctors, nurses, social workers, physical therapists, and volunteer workers.

PAYING FOR HOSPICE

Paul and Alice had excellent health insurance through their state's employee union, but even without private insurance, hospice care would have been readily available. Of all the medical services available in the United States, hospice comes the closest to being fully funded.

In most states, many sources pay for hospice care. These sources include Medicare, Medicaid, most private insurance plans, the Department of Veterans Affairs, health maintenance organizations (HMOs), and other managed care organizations. To receive payment from Medicare, the agency must be approved by Medicare to provide hospice services.

Home hospice care usually costs less than care in hospitals, nursing homes, or other institutional settings. These cost savings have provided a strong incentive to fully fund hospice care. Hospice, in turn, owes a measure of its success to the financial support it receives from government and private sources.

When necessary, hospice programs charge patients according to their ability to pay. The goal of hospice—which has been largely accomplished—is to make hospice services available to all persons regardless of ability to pay.

HOSPICE AND THE
COMPASSION PROTOCOL

If you are clearly terminally ill, you can easily turn to hospice as an excellent source of palliative care, that is, care that provides pain control, symptom management, and emotional and spiritual support during the last days of life. Your doctor will refer you and arrange for hospice service to begin, just as Dr. Fitzpatrick did for Paul.

However, end-of-life comfort and support from hospice might be more difficult for two other groups of people who use the Compassion Protocol to choose a natural death: the sentient elderly and the demented. These two groups would benefit from hospice care during their final days just as much as the terminally ill would.

People in these two groups who follow the five simple steps of the Compassion Protocol can ask their doctor to refer them for hospice care as part of implementing the Contract for Compassionate Care. There may be times when a physician believes a person will have longer than six months to live, but generally anyone employing the contract should qualify immediately for hospice referral. If you are ready to cease curative care, stop your usual medications, and allow a natural death, you will qualify for hospice. You, too, may be allowed a natural death sooner rather than later if that is your choice.

CHAPTER TWELVE

EVERYONE'S WORST FEAR: THE NURSING HOME

Throughout this book we have assumed that placement in a nursing home is not something anyone would choose except as a last resort. In fact, our position is that for many of us it is literally a fate worse than death. This is consistent with what many in our generation have told us: "I'd rather go peacefully in my sleep than end up in a nursing home."

DR. FITZPATRICK RELATES THE STORY OF SEAN O'CONNOR: A REGRETTABLY COMMON NURSING HOME EXPERIENCE

Sean O'Connor spent the first half of his life as a heroin addict. During this period he had very limited contact with his parents because his addiction increasingly took away human relationships, and this was in addition to all the other wreckage of an addict's life.

In his early fifties Sean got clean and stayed clean. He became my patient to get treatment for the ravaging effects that his addiction had dealt his body: off-the-chart high liver enzymes, a stomach ulcer, chronic trouble sleeping, and the like. Without the constant presence of heroin in his bloodstream, his body began to heal. We worked on diet and exercise programs. I found Sean to be a willing and hardworking patient.

One of the more valuable gifts that sobriety gave him was drawing close to the parents he loved deeply. He was especially close to his father, whom he described as his hero—the most admirable man he had the privilege of knowing.

WAREHOUSES FOR THE ELDERLY

Three years into Sean's sobriety his father suffered a stroke. While his cognition was not affected, he had weakness and difficulty moving the left side of his body. His left arm and leg also ached uncomfortably.

After five days the hospital told Sean they could do no more for his father, and Sean made arrangements for his father to be transferred to a nursing home for rehabilitation, with the hope that he would regain enough function to return to his own home.

Sean visited his father at the nursing home the very next day. He found his father slumped over in a wheelchair. A seatbelt-like strap held his body in place. An orderly was tugging on the strap to tighten it in an effort to move his father into a more upright position. The orderly's tugging didn't straighten him in the wheelchair; it only held him more tightly in his slumped position. Worse yet, his father was now having trouble speaking. He was mostly unresponsive. Sean wasn't even sure his father knew him.

Sean settled his father more comfortably back in his bed, where his father curled into a fetal position. Sean was angry and dismayed. How could his father have deteriorated so much in just one day?

He met with the nursing home management and care team, where he learned that his father had received no physical therapy. They explained that his father's progression since the time of his stroke was not encouraging. The most they could do for him at this point was try to make him as comfortable as possible.

Sean visited his father every day that week. He spent an hour or so moving and massaging his father's limbs. He also helped his father sit on the edge of the bed and put his feet on the floor. His father remained drowsy and glassy-eyed.

One day Sean visited his father on the way to work, since he knew he would have to work late that evening. It was the first time he had seen his father that early in the day. A nurse came in with a tiny paper cup filled with pills—his father's morning meds. Sean asked what they were. He didn't recognize any of them except for Vicodin, which he knew was a powerful narcotic pain reliever.

When asked why his father was on Vicodin, the nurse checked his chart and reported that it was because of the ache in his left arm and leg. He was receiving two Vicodin every four hours when he was awake. At this point Sean called me. He was terribly upset and needed a reality check as to what he could expect from his father at this point.

I called the staff doctor at the nursing home and then met Sean there the following evening. In concert with the staff doctor, we decided to discontinue the Vicodin and see what kind of pain level we were dealing with.

Two days later I received a message on my answering machine from Sean. He was speaking rapidly, eager to share the good news. He had arrived at the nursing home that evening and was amazed to find his father sitting up and eating dinner. It turned out that his father had been the victim of overly aggressive pain management. Without the Vicodin he was awake and mentally his usual self, anxious to get on with his rehabilitation and to return home. His arm and leg still ached, but with plain Tylenol the pain was manageable. The change in his father was nothing short of miraculous.

Sean and I talked later that evening. When Sean thought about what had happened, he became increasingly angry. He said his experience had shown him that nursing homes were nothing more than warehouses for the elderly and infirm who were marking time until death. If he hadn't been proactive with his father's care, his father would still be curled in a fetal position with dazed, glassy eyes, completely unresponsive. Because of Sean's intervention, his father was given physical therapy twice daily. Within a week he was walking with a walker. In two more weeks he went home. His condition continued to improve.

Sean summarized the effects of his experience by saying, "If I ever have to be placed in a nursing home, I'm bringing my pistol with me so that I have the option of moving on." In Sean's opinion, all nursing home patrons should similarly be allowed to opt out. His final comment on his experience? "There are fates worse than death."

UNDERSTANDING YOUR
NURSING HOME OPTION

Nursing home care is a large and thriving industry. Currently there are more than eighteen thousand nursing homes in the United States, with an aggregate of 1.9 million beds. More than 1.6 million people reside in nursing homes on any given day. The average length of stay is about ten months.

Like most things, nursing homes come in a variety of shapes and colors. They are, ideally, a place for the elderly who can no longer care for themselves to live out their days in comfort, safety, and companionship. In practice, this ideal is often unrealized.

Among those who have been forced to place loved ones in long-term care there is often dissatisfaction with the treatment provided. Many nursing homes suffer from chronic understaffing, resulting in one poorly paid, poorly trained aide being asked to provide full care for up to thirty-five clients for eight solid hours. If the clients were able to get to the bathroom by themselves or feed themselves or perform other simple activities of daily living, they would probably still be living in their own homes. Instead, they are dependent on care for every need, and that care is often slow, reluctant, resentful, or nonexistent.

Patients most often find their way into nursing homes from the hospital. The reasons for hospitalization may include a needed surgery, pneumonia, a new compression fracture of the spine, an injury from a fall, or increased congestive heart failure. These conditions result in a turn for the worse in someone who previously was living alone and coping adequately. The patient is admitted to the hospital for treatment of the acute condition.

During treatment there is an evaluation by the hospital social worker and a conference with the family. This is the point at which it may be decided that Mom (Dad, Sis, Aunt, or Uncle) needs a week or two in the nursing home to gather her strength again. Months later she may still be there, having lost hope of returning home.

NURSING HOMES: A GROWTH BUSINESS

Four major social changes have conspired to create the rapid growth of nursing home admissions. The first is the obvious fact that people are living longer: Life expectancy at birth is now above eighty, and for the current elderly, survival past the age of sixty-five gives them a good chance of survival to ninety. This is due to the fact that this generation has taken better care of themselves, eating well and living active lives, coupled with the successful treatment of cardiac risk factors such as diabetes, hypertension, and cholesterol elevations. Survival to extreme old age carries with it increased risk of the mental deterioration of dementia and the physical deterioration of osteoporosis and osteoarthritis, forcing many of the extreme elderly into nursing homes.

The second major change is in our social mobility. Family members are by far the most common caregivers for the extreme elderly. Yet children often move away from the town in which they grew up, leaving their elderly parents with no family members in their local vicinity. When Mom or Dad needs help, there is no one to step in and provide in-home care.

A third factor in the continuing growth of the nursing home

industry will be the aging of the baby boomers. This demographic group has impacted each societal marker it has encountered, from Dr. Spock to natural childbirth to diet and exercise regimes, ad infinitum. We believe the natural death movement will be the next life event the baby boomers will re-create, with profound and positive consequences for our society's approach to the end of life.

The final change has been to our societal norms. Since the latter part of the twentieth century it has been socially acceptable to place our elderly and infirm parents in a place of specialized care. Various factors have contributed to this development: the two-wage-earner family, in which no one is home during the day to provide care for an ailing family member; the rise of youth culture, beginning with "trust no one over thirty"; and the emergence of elder care as a medical specialty, to name a few.

As the baby boom generation increasingly encounters the unsatisfactory solution of nursing home "warehouses," home health care alternatives will increasingly emerge as a viable option.

THE HOME HEALTH CARE ALTERNATIVE

Home health care provides an alternative to the nursing home for those who can afford it or who have had the resources to purchase adequate long-term care insurance. Dr. Fitzpatrick has never had a patient who *wanted* to go into a nursing home. Whenever possible she has helped her elderly, infirm patients navigate the paperwork hurdles required to take maximum advantage of services available in the home. One goal of the Compassion Protocol is to encourage and support people who wish to avail themselves of home health care rather than hospitalization or institutionalization.

The elderly who manage to stay in their own home or are able to move in with other family members thrive and recuperate far faster than those placed in nursing homes. They remain in familiar surroundings and are able to continue much of their usual activity. Most important, they retain the ability to control their schedules and activities, making some small but very important choices on their own every day. Allowing this minor level of independence is extremely important to the elderly, though it provides significant challenges to caregivers.

Arranging for in-home care requires a team approach. A social worker should be made available by the patient's physician or by the hospital. Additional resources may also be found through the state Office on Aging or the local Area Agency on Aging. An excellent resource is the American Association of Retired Persons (AARP), whose Caregiver Resource Kit is a valuable help in finding local services.

Volunteer help may be available through senior centers or the Area Agency on Aging. This can include in-home visitors who provide help with reading, writing, shopping, or just companionship. Meals on Wheels will deliver one hot meal daily to homebound clients. Transportation services may be available for trips to the doctor.

With physician referral, many insurance programs will pay for home health aides or even visiting nurses if that level of care is required. Physical therapy can usually be arranged in the home.

Some areas may also have geriatric care managers available to those who can afford them.

Home health care coupled with your careful, informed choice of a nursing home can achieve an optimal outcome. The next section provides an example of helpful and humane end-of-life care.

WHEN THE SYSTEM WORKS: DR. FITZPATRICK TELLS THE STORY OF SALLY FOREST

One of my favorite patients during my four years in family practice was Sally Forest, a spry eighty-nine-year-old, when I first met her, who was a dwindling ninety-three-year-old when I left my practice. During our four years together she went from living independently in her own home to being bedridden and in need of twenty-four-hour care.

Sally never worked outside of the home but had a master's degree in economics of which she was very proud. Her husband was a dentist, and her three children were well-educated professionals. One son works in Silicon Valley, one is a dentist in Kansas City, and her daughter is a physician in Phoenix.

During the four years I knew Sally, her children never visited her. (Lest the reader find this shocking, it is, regrettably, far more common than one would think.) During the first two years I treated her, she made two carefully planned visits to her children. She was very proud that she was able to get a limousine to pick her up at home, take her to the airport, and help her get her wheelchair to the terminal. She had a third visit planned for most of the last two years but could never quite make it happen.

Her husband died about six months before I met her. On her visits to me she was accompanied by Barbara, whom she paid for four hours of in-home care daily. Barbara had no formal training but worked full-time as a caregiver for Sally and two other elderly women in their own homes. She was in her late sixties and treated Sally like a sister.

Sally walked with great difficulty using two canes. Her spine had shortened by eight inches, her height decreasing from her usual five feet nine inches to just over five feet. Her spine was twisted with scoliosis in both the upper and lower back, and every movement caused her pain. She had lived a very healthy lifestyle and had suffered no heart or lung problems. She hadn't been in the hospital since her gallbladder surgery thirty years earlier.

I treated Sally for hypertension, osteoporosis, osteoarthritis, bladder incontinence, and chronic back pain. She always asked for my last appointment in the morning, knowing that after her formal appointment we would visit for at least half an hour and often an hour. About half of our time together was spent reviewing her medications, her carefully prepared list of blood pressure readings, and her pain journal. During the other half we just visited, an activity we both found very therapeutic. I saw her once a month.

During her first winter as my patient, Sally caught a bad cold and over two weeks became increasingly weak and short of breath. I saw her first on the second day of her illness, when she just had the sniffles, sneezes, and a cough. Her lungs were clear and her breathing was fine, but she was very worried about becoming sicker. I recommended nothing but rest, good nutrition with very careful attention to low-salt meals, some extra vitamin C just in case, echinacea, some cough medicine with a narcotic in it to let her get some good rest, and, of course, lots of chicken soup.

On the second visit four days later, she was having more trouble walking and hadn't been able to get out of bed by herself for two days. She had an appropriate fear of falling, given her difficulties with back pain even on a good day. Barbara was staying eight hours each day instead of her usual four and had found a friend who could help out on weekends. Her visit that day marked the first time I saw Sally in a wheelchair.

Sally told me she was staying in bed during her hours alone, wearing a diaper and contenting herself with the TV remote control and some prepared snacks and water. She was still her usual alert and perky self. She had no increased pain since she wasn't doing any walking. She denied any shortness of breath, but her respiratory rate had increased and her oxygen saturation at rest had fallen to 89 percent. Her lungs had some rales at both bases that didn't clear with a cough. Although she had a low-grade fever during the first forty-eight hours of her symptoms, she had not had any fever during the previous four days. I checked a complete blood count (CBC), looking for evidence of infection, and it was normal. A chest X-ray showed her small lung cage, compromised by her collapsed spine, and an enlarged heart that had not changed since an X-ray two years earlier. Her electrolytes were fine.

I talked with her during that second visit about staying in the hospital for a few days, mostly in order to receive oxygen and good respiratory care. She was adamant that she would be okay at home. She was eating well and sleeping well, and was firmly convinced the hospital would make her sicker, not better. I arranged to have an oxygen tank delivered to her home so that she could get 2 liters of oxygen by nasal cannula. It was Friday, so I made sure that both she and Barbara knew about my weekend plans and what to do if she got worse. She made an appointment to see me again on Monday.

But when Monday came, she was too weak to make it to her appointment. Instead, Barbara called an ambulance, and Sally came to the ER for treatment. The doctor there called me, and I saw Sally in the ER. The most obvious change in her was her grooming: Her usually perfect makeup was missing, and her hair was limp and dirty. But her eyes still had their sparkle, and her smile was still warm.

She greeted me with humor and an apology: "Hi, Doc. This washed-out old lady thought she'd visit you in bed this time, just to see if your bedside manner is as pleasant as your office persona." Her breathing was labored, and it took her four breaths to say this one sentence.

Barbara was seated next to her and looked almost as ill as Sally. She had caught Sally's cold and was on the second day of it, miserable with a fever, nasal congestion, and a harsh dry cough. She had been spending most of every day with Sally and was exhausted.

I hospitalized Sally that day with a diagnosis of pneumonia and congestive heart failure based on her labs and X-ray. She had a low-grade fever and very poor air movement in her lungs. She had stopped eating and drinking, feeling too nauseated, and was also slightly dehydrated. She needed good respiratory treatment, intravenous antibiotics, nutritional support, and twenty-four-hour care for safety. I took her complete lack of argument as a measure of how ill she felt.

By the third day of hospitalization Sally's fever was gone, her lungs sounded better, and her numbers all looked fine. She was ready to leave the hospital—but she remained extremely weak, sleeping most of every day. Of special concern was her inability to perform any of her daily activities on her own, calling into question her ability to live independently.

The patient care coordinator offered to find Sally a nursing home for a few weeks of rehabilitation. She urgently made the point that Sally no longer qualified for hospitalization even though she obviously could not be alone at home.

A Difficult Conversation

Sally and I had that difficult talk I've had far too many times with elderly patients. She appeared to be asleep when I approached her bed. Her eyelids fluttered open when I lifted her hand, and she smiled at me.

"Hey, Doc, I guess I'm going to live through this after all. I'm feeling almost human again."

I responded, "I think you're doing better, but you're a long way from well. It's time for you to leave the hospital. We're not really doing anything for you now that can't be done somewhere else, and Medicare regulations say you have to leave today or tomorrow."

"Fine with me," she said. "Nothing personal, but I don't really like this hotel very much."

"So what are we going to do with you?"

"Well, Doc, get me my slippers, and I'll dance on out of here. This will let you take care of really sick people." She started to laugh, and it turned into a coughing spell that left her exhausted, gasping, and nearly unconscious. I waited until she was breathing comfortably again before continuing.

"Has Barbara been in today?"

"No. I haven't seen her since I got here. I hope she's home taking care of herself and getting better."

"Sally, I don't think you should go home alone. Even with Barbara checking in on you, I think you're just too sick to be home alone. You're so weak, you can barely even roll over in bed by yourself."

She was suddenly the most alert she had been in three days. She mustered the strength to sit up and said, with a strong voice and more than a little bit of anger, "You are not putting me in a nursing home. Don't even think about it."

"But, Sally, you'll have help there if you need it, and I hate to think of your being alone when you're so sick."

"Why? What's the worst that could happen? I might die? You know I'd rather do that than go to a nursing home. We've had this conversation before, Doc."

"No, Sally, it's not dying that I worry about. It's your being alone and needing help and not being able to get it."

"Barbara will be there every morning at eight o'clock. I'll only be alone overnight. I still have the oxygen. As you said, you're not doing much for me here anymore. I'll just go home and keep getting better in my own bed, thank you. What's wrong with that?"

Indeed, I had no good answer for her. She had an unusually strong will and determination, and a very clear picture of her wants and needs.

I confirmed with Barbara that she would be available to Sally during the day. Barbara was still coughing but felt on the mend and able to cope with six to eight hours of caregiving daily. I arranged for a visiting nurse to make a house call daily for at least two weeks, and for a physical therapist to visit three times a week to start working with Sally on regaining her ability to walk.

AN EXAMPLE OF INCREASED CHOICE AND CONTROL AT THE END OF LIFE

I gave it at least a fifty-fifty chance that Sally would deteriorate during the next few days. If improvement was slow in coming, Sally might need the specialized care that nursing homes can give. But I was very willing to comply with her wishes to avoid the nursing home, at least in the first instance.

Barbara checked in with me after two days and said Sally seemed to be slowly getting a little stronger. Sally wasn't even close to walking on her own yet, but she was comfortable and her vital signs were stable. She was very happy to be in her own bed and home.

Sally returned to my office after two weeks, still in a wheelchair but with makeup intact and hair in its usual stylish (for the 1950s) bob. She seemed almost her usual self, cheerful, talkative, purposeful in her movements, and very direct in her speech. She hadn't yet managed to walk by herself, but she was continuing physical therapy.

She had reluctantly agreed to start learning how to transfer herself from the bed to the wheelchair, in case she was never able to walk independently again. The visiting nurse had just discharged Sally from home health care, meaning that Medicare was no longer available for keeping Sally at home with adequate home health care.

It was three months before Sally walked into my office with her two canes again. She laughed about working so hard to be able to cause herself so much pain: Sitting in the wheelchair was much easier than walking. But she valued quality of life and considered independent ambulation an essential part of life. I was very proud of her and wished I could bottle up some of her personal strength and determination to give to some of my other patients.

REFLECTIONS

Sally was a woman with adequate resources, sufficient mental ability, and admirable strength of spirit. These factors, plus her ability to clearly state her preferences, meant she was able to avoid placement in a nursing home. It is worth noting that most people in her circumstances, suffering from severe acute illness, would have been forced into a nursing home for, at a minimum, a period of recuperation. Sally left the hospital to return to her own home full of gratitude and determination to succeed.

Sally also maintained her financial independence by staying

home. The average cost of a nursing home bed is about $6,000 per month. These costs would have come out of her pocket until she used up all her savings. In fact, most people who are admitted to a nursing home run out of money and become dependent on Medicaid.

Precipitating events—those that cause a patient to move into a nursing home—may include one or more of these conditions: a needed surgery, pneumonia, a new compression fracture of the spine, an injury from a fall, or increased congestive heart failure. Once ensconced in the nursing home, financial resources are often depleted within six months. Sally had no long-term care insurance, and it would have hurt her horribly to have to take a federal government handout.

Sally's success at home was very dependent on the team approach—the combined skills of the in-home caregiver, the visiting nurse, and the physical therapist. It is usually a family member or visiting social worker who works to coordinate the various in-home services that are essential to remaining in one's home. Sally's experience shows that the patient's own determination can be sufficient to manage the necessary resources for in-home care.

It is no accident that most of this chapter on nursing homes deals with how to avoid nursing home care through various home health options. Simply put, we have never encountered a person who actively wanted to move into a nursing home. Therefore, a key element of the Compassion Protocol is aimed at facilitating your ability to remain in your own home, cared for as you want to be, for as long as possible.

The Contract for Compassionate Care is a binding legal document, and we urge you to make use of it. It can be used by anyone at any age. The next chapter, entitled Looking Ahead, discusses how our contract fits into the current legal forms and practices, and it summarizes some of the changes we hope the Compassion Protocol can accomplish.

CHAPTER THIRTEEN

LOOKING AHEAD

We are suggesting substantial changes in the way death is considered and accomplished in this country. We hope the stories in this book have shown why we feel change is needed. Natural death is what most of us want: to slip away quietly in our sleep, in our own home, with our loved ones nearby. It is our hope that the option of a natural death, found by withdrawing from curative care, will rescue many people and their families from the pain of advanced Alzheimer's or the debility of extreme old age.

The Compassion Protocol and its Contract for Compassionate Care are the tools we propose to allow us all to find that natural death when the time comes. These are new tools in a field that is ripe with forms already available. In the past thirty years, legislatures and courts have addressed repeatedly the substance and wording of Advance Directives. Our form simplifies that language while retaining the substance.

Our Contract for Compassionate Care is very similar to the POLST forms developed originally in Oregon and now recognized in many states. However, there are important differences.

Our contract can be completed proactively. In fact, we hope everyone of every age will complete our form in order to plan in advance the control and choices wanted at the end of life. Our form lets you state what you *don't* want at the end of life in terms of medical intervention because we see the withdrawal from care as the road to a natural death.

In contrast, the POLST form is designed to be used only at the end of life, not proactively. Although it has been wrongly interpreted by caregivers as requiring a terminal diagnosis, it is in fact meant to be implemented immediately at the time of signing. It cannot be used to indicate choices that you want to make (or you want your Health Care Decision Maker to make for you) at some point in the future—as an illness progresses, for instance.

The struggle by the originators of the POLST form to gain full acceptance of and compliance with POLST directives has had very beneficial results. Because of their work, withdrawal from curative care is a realistic option already in many parts of the country. When used properly, the POLST form allows the elderly, or the demented through their Health Care Decision Maker, to withdraw from curative care. It does not, however, allow young and healthy people to state their preference for withdrawal of curative care proactively.

There are Advance Directive forms that can be used proactively; that is, you can state what care you *do* want when you are in a coma or terminally ill. However, these Advance Directives are particularly ineffective at helping patients who have dementia or other nonterminal but progressive illness find natural death in the earlier stages of their disease. In addition to the limitation of their scope, we find these forms cumbersome, confusing, and complex. They were designed by lawyers, and legal help is usually needed to understand them.

The complexity of these forms is not needed. Remember that the Supreme Court has determined you have the right to make your own health care decisions, and no one can interfere with that right. All you need is a simple statement of your preferences, such as our contract or the POLST form. You do not need a twenty-page Advance Directive and Living Will.

If you are worried about a slow decline from Alzheimer's or other debilitating illness, neither Advance Directives nor POLST forms allow you to choose to withdraw from curative care at a time in the future as your dementia progresses. That is the main difference between our form and other available forms. Only the Compassion Protocol allows you to state your choice for withdrawal from care at some point in the course of Alzheimer's.

Our simple Contract for Compassionate Care, which combines the POLST choices with the option to make the choices proactive, complies with the findings of the Supreme Court in the landmark cases we discussed in this book. It lets you control your end-of-life care as only you can. The Supreme Court has given you that absolute control. Unless someone can challenge your mental soundness at the time of signing our contract, it is likely to hold up to any court challenge. (Remember to videotape your signing.)

Health Care Decision Makers for those already trapped in the fog of Alzheimer's dementia will probably wonder how the Compassion Protocol can help their loved ones. These loved ones did not have the chance to complete the Compassion Protocol while still mentally competent, and it might seem as if they do not have the option for withdrawal of curative care at some point in their illness's progression. You must remember that you still have the legal right to make that choice for them if they ever told you in a "clear and convincing" way that they would prefer an early death to the long, slow decline of dementia.

If you know with certainty, from things they said to you while they were still competent, that your loved ones would want you to keep them home and comfortable the next time they have a possible exit event, then you have the legal right to do that. You do not have to take them to the hospital for curative care. In fact, it is your obligation as the Health Care Decision Maker to do what you think they would want done if they were still able to make their own decisions.

You should be able to talk over that choice with other family members. Remind them that you are just carrying out the patient's own wishes as he or she stated them to you. If there are siblings or other family members who still fight for full treatment, we recommend a mediator. Outsiders are often better at resolving difficult family disagreements.

Whatever form you use to indicate your end-of-life choices, we still emphasize that the conversations you have with your family and caregiver are more important than the form. It is our strong hope that this book will facilitate conversations within families about death and dying. If there is someone in your family who is descending into frailty, debility, or dementia, we hope our book helps you begin a conversation with that person about the choices that exist for end-of-life care.

We are sure that many people, given the choice, will reach a point where natural death is preferable to continued life. We hope this book will help them find that choice. As the baby boomers reach their old age, they will look for new ways to deal with old problems. They are unlikely to find an alternative to death, but they will at least be able to replace the mechanized hospital death with a natural, peaceful ending to life.

Appendix A

Contract for Compassionate Care

CONTRACT FOR COMPASSIONATE CARE This is my doctor order sheet. It is based on my medical condition and wishes. It summarizes my treatment choices for end-of-life care and sets forth the timing options for when my treatment choices will go into effect. It also appoints my Health Care Decision Maker.	Last Name
	First Name/Middle Initial
	Date of Birth

I. RESUSCITATION ORDER: If I have no pulse and am not breathing (initial ONE):

_____ Resuscitate   _____ Do NOT Resuscitate

II. MEDICAL INTERVENTION AND TIMING ORDER: I choose the following limitations to medical intervention at the end of my life (initial ALL that apply):

_____ **Comfort Care Only:** I choose to refuse medical intervention except as may be needed to provide comfort. Comfort measures are to be used where I live or reside. I am not to be sent to the hospital or emergency room again unless comfort measures fail.

_____ I do not want to receive antibiotics again.

_____ I do not want to continue my usual medications.

_____ I do not want food and water except as I choose it or request it. No intravenous fluids or feeding tubes.

I want the Orders chosen above to apply when: (initial ALL that apply):

_____ Immediately

_____ I am close to death

_____ I have an advanced progressive illness

_____ I am permanently unconscious

_____ I am experiencing extraordinary suffering

_____ I have dementia and have passed certain benchmarks known to my Health Care Decision Maker. Some of those benchmarks are:

_____

_____

_____

III. APPOINTMENT OF HEALTH CARE DECISION MAKER: I appoint

_____ as my Health Care Decision Maker. I appoint
_____ as my alternate Decision Maker. I authorize
my Health Care Decision Maker to direct my health care when I cannot do so. I authorize my Decision Maker to implement my options for withdrawal from medical intervention under circumstances known to him/her as best representing my own wishes.

IV. SIGNATURE

I, _____, ask that my doctors, other health care providers, family, friends, and all others follow my wishes as communicated by my Health Care Decision Maker.

_____

Signature   Date

_____

Address

WITNESS STATEMENT: I, the witness, declare that the person who signed this form is personally known to me, that he/she signed it in my presence, and that he/she appears to be of sound mind and under no duress, fraud, or undue influence.

_____		_____	
Signature of Witness #1	Date	Signature of Witness #2	Date
_____		_____	
Printed Name of Witness		Printed Name of Witness	
_____		_____	
Address		Address	

PHYSICIAN SIGNATURE: I acknowledge that _____ has discussed this form with me and confirmed that it represents his/her wishes for health care at the end of life. I agree to comply with his/her wishes.

_____

Physician Signature   Date

_____

Printed Name of Physician

_____

Address

V. REVIEW OF THIS CONTRACT

Review Date	Reviewer	Location of Review	Review Outcome	
			__ No Change __ Form Voided	__ New Form Completed
			__ No Change __ Form Voided	__ New Form Completed
			__ No Change __ Form Voided	__ New Form Completed

SEND FORM WITH PERSON WHENEVER TRANSFERRED OR DISCHARGED

Appendix B

———

Tools for the Compassion Protocol

I. THE COMPASSION
PROTOCOL WORKSHEET

Before proceeding with any part of this contract, it is important
to understand your motives and eliminate depressive disorders
as a motivating factor in your decision. Answer each of the five
questions below as best you can. There is space provided after
each question so that you can write out your response. Answer
the questions with as much specificity as you can.

1. Am I just depressed?

_____

_____

_____

_____

_____

2. Is it possible life could get better again?

_____

_____

_____

_____

_____

3. Do I have any important unfinished business?

_____

_____

_____

_____

4. Do I still enjoy waking up in the morning?

_____

_____

_____

_____

5. Am I ready to let death happen?

_____

_____

_____

_____

_____

II. MY PROS AND CONS LIST

REASONS TO CONTINUE LIVING

REASONS TO WANT A NATURAL DEATH TO OCCUR SOONER RATHER THAN LATER

_____

_____

_____

_____

_____

_____

_____

_____

_____

_____

_____

_____

_____

_____

_____

_____

_____

_____

_____

_____

_____

_____

_____

_____

_____

_____

Glossary

Some terms and definitions in this glossary are from *Stedman's Medical Dictionary*, 28th ed. (Baltimore: Lippincott Williams & Wilkins, 2006).

active-assisted suicide: voluntary termination of one's own life with active assistance

acute illness: illness that begins and ends in a short period of time

apnea: absence of breathing

apneic: suffering from apnea

ascites: massive swelling of the belly from fluid leaking out of the bowel because of the buildup of pressure behind the nonfunctioning liver

to bag her/him: to force air into lungs that are not functioning by placing a tight mask over the mouth and forcing air into it

carbon dioxide narcosis: level of decreased mental function caused by the buildup of carbon dioxide in the blood

catabolic state: condition of increased metabolism often resulting in weight loss as more calories are burned up (usually by a cancer) than are consumed

code: term used in hospitals to describe an emergency, usually cardiac arrest, requiring immediate response

code four: patient arrives in an ambulance with lights and sirens

code one: patient arrives in an ambulance but is not in extremis, so the ambulance is not using lights and siren

comfort care: medical care directed at relieving pain and suffering and maintaining comfort, but not treating any acute illness

congestive heart failure: condition where a weak and tired heart is easily overwhelmed, causing fluid to build up in legs and lungs, causing shortness of breath and ankle swelling

CPR: cardiopulmonary resuscitation: the use of chest compressions and mouth-to-mouth breathing for someone who has no pulse or respirations

curative care: medical care designed to cure an acute illness

Do Not Resuscitate (DNR) order: an instruction signed by your doctor that you do not want heroic measures used to resuscitate you, including CPR, if you stop breathing or your heart stops beating

drug toxicity: the state of suffering ill effects from taking too much of a drug

dysrhythmia: any abnormality in the rate, regularity, or sequence of cardiac activation

electrolyte imbalance: abnormality of the concentration of salts (especially potassium, sodium, chloride, and carbonate) in the blood

euthanasia: (1) a quiet, painless death; (2) the intentional putting to death of a person with an incurable or painful disease, intended as an act of mercy

exit event: a treatable acute illness that, if left untreated, might cause a person's death

fasciculations: small rapid tremors in a muscle resulting from injury or lack of oxygen

grand mal seizure: a generalized seizure characterized by loss of consciousness, often a fall to the ground, muscle rigidity, and then clonic muscle and limb twitching

Health Care Decision Maker: person chosen by you to make health care decisions for you if you become unable to make them yourself

hospice: an institution that provides a centralized program of palliative and supportive services to dying people and their families, in the form of physical, psychological, social, and spiritual care; such services are provided by an interdisciplinary team of professionals and volunteers who are available in the home and in specialized inpatient settings

hydration: generally, a measure of water content; medically, a measure of a person's fluid balance

hypercarbic drive: the stimulus to inhale and exhale resulting from increased carbon dioxide in the blood

hypoxia: below-normal levels of oxygen in the blood

hypoxic damage: tissue damage resulting from a period of hypoxia

hypoxic drive: the stimulus to inhale and exhale resulting from low oxygen content in the blood

ICU: Intensive Care Unit; a hospital facility for provision of intensive nursing and medical care of critically ill patients

in extremis: exhibiting extreme medical symptoms, usually implying the risk of death

intubating: inserting a tube into the lungs for control of breathing

IV: intravenous, meaning within a vein or veins

life support: use of artificial, externally applied means to keep a person alive

Living Will: a legal document in which you state your wishes regarding life support if you are terminally ill, permanently unconscious, or in a coma; it also addresses whether you want to be kept alive with a respirator or a feeding tube.

loading dose: a comparatively large dose given at the beginning of treatment to start getting the effect of a drug quickly

metastatic: spreading of a malignant tumor from one part of the body to another

nasal cannula: small plastic tube that delivers oxygen through a person's nose

palliative care: care aimed at relieving symptoms without curing the disease

paracentesis: removal of fluid from a body cavity by insertion of a needle or catheter

pathological fracture: fracture occurring at a site in the bone weakened by preexisting disease, such as neoplasm or necrosis

PEEP (Positive End-Expiratory Pressure) mask: externally placed mask that makes a tight seal on the face and allows delivery of positive pressure during respiration to help open damaged lungs

persistent vegetative state: prolonged state of impaired consciousness, usually following head trauma, in which a person is incapable of voluntary or purposeful acts and only responds reflexively to painful stimuli

physician-assisted suicide: voluntary termination of one's own life by administration of a lethal substance with the direct or indirect assistance of a physician. It is to be distinguished from the withholding or discontinuance of life-support measures in terminal or vegetative states so that the patient dies of the underlying illness and from administration of narcotic analgesics in terminal cancer, which may indirectly hasten death.

Physician Orders for Life-Sustaining Treatment (POLST) form: a contract between you and your doctor in which the doctor agrees to the care you will receive at the end of life

Power of Attorney for Health Care: legal document in which you appoint a family member or friend as your Health Care Decision Maker. He or she will tell the doctors what your wishes are if you are mentally incapacitated, permanently unconscious, or in a coma.

rales: abnormal breath sounds heard on ausculation of breath sounds, indicating fluid or infection in the lungs

respiratory arrest: death or near death caused by cessation of breathing

reversible component: treatable and curable part of an illness

scoliosis: curvature of the spine

sentient (sentient elderly): with intact cognition and memory

sinus tachycardia: regular rapid heartbeat

somatic complaints: physical symptoms

status epilepticus: seizure prolonged for at least thirty minutes

subcutaneous fat: adipose tissue; what is usually meant by "meat on his/her bones"

tonic-clonic seizure: another term for grand mal seizure

Total Parenteral Nutrition (TPN): nutrition supported entirely by liquid administered by tube

vasoconstriction: narrowing of the blood vessels

workup: evaluation